The
United
States
and
China

The United States and China

The Next Decade

EDITED BY

A. DOAK BARNETT

AND

EDWIN O. REISCHAUER

WITH THE ASSISTANCE OF

LOIS DOUGAN TRETIAK

PRAEGER PUBLISHERS
New York · Washington · London

PRAEGER PUBLISHERS
111 Fourth Avenue, New York, N.Y. 10003, U.S.A.
5, Cromwell Place, London, S.W.7, England

Published in the United States of America in 1970
by Praeger Publishers, Inc.

Printed in the United States of America

This book is dedicated to the memory of Cecil A. Thomas, first Executive Director of the National Committee on United States—China Relations, whose inspiration and untiring efforts were in large measure responsible for the formation of the Committee and the organization of its national convocation.

CONTENTS

PREFACE

The first national convocation on "The United States and China: The Next Decade" was held in New York City on March 20–21, 1969. It was sponsored by the National Committee on United States–China Relations and was attended by a large and varied group—some 2,500 people from many different professions and areas. The interest the convocation evoked is an important indication of the growing belief in the United States that the issues and problems involved in America's China policy deserve far greater attention and discussion than they have received in the past.

This is a most opportune time for a thorough public examination of China policy issues and the policy options open to the United States. Twenty years have passed since a Communist regime was established on the Chinese mainland. Today, in China—and, in fact, in Asia as a whole—significant processes of change are under way. And, in the United States, the Nixon Administration has an opportunity to take a fresh look at all the major issues of national policy facing this country—including China policy.

The National Committee on United States–China Relations, which has sponsored this volume as well as the convocation, is dedicated to the task of public education on the problems and issues involved in U.S. relations with China. It was established in 1966 as a nonpartisan, independent, educational organization, with a membership representing a wide variety of Americans in the business, labor, professional, religious, and academic communities and covering a broad spectrum of political and policy views. The Committee itself does not take any position on policy issues. Its purpose is to engage leaders and citizens throughout the country in intelligent, ongoing public discussion of China and U.S. policy problems and to try to help increase American understanding of this important and complex area of U.S. foreign relations.

The Committee has sponsored, and will continue to sponsor, a variety of programs—including community leader and professional group seminars throughout the country. At several major universities, graduate students studying East Asian affairs are affiliated with the Committee and are developing various types of programs. The Committee has provided a range of information services and has published a number of informational guides to assist those interested in serious study of problems.

The Committee firmly believes that, if the United States is to make intelligent decisions on what its national interests are and what its national policies should be, it is essential that the American public be fully informed about the issues and problems. We feel that broader dissemination of the statements made by speakers at the convocation will contribute toward this end, and it is our hope that this book will help to raise the level of public knowledge and understanding of how best to approach the problems of United States–China relations in the decade ahead.

A. DOAK BARNETT
*Chairman, National Committee
on United States–China Relations, 1968–69*

A NOTE TO SET THE SCENE

The March, 1969, convocation, "The United States and China: The Next Decade," out of which this book grew, was neither an academic meeting of China scholars nor a two-day conversation of people "interested in China." Rather it brought together a variety of approaches to the subjects of United States–China relations and American China policy: those of the scholar, the trader, the journalist, people who must view China from afar and others who are able to see "close-up," officials who represent Washington and people who look at China and the United States from the different vantage points of other capitals.

The conference was noteworthy for its quality of "learned men thinking aloud." It was designed to look at current problems and future alternatives for action rather than to take a backward look at the history of United States–China relations, although many speakers indicated the historical perspectives from which they spoke. All the speakers seemed to sense the immediacy of the issues surrounding the Sino-American relationship, but while some called for action and American initiatives, others cautioned against change or haste.

To permit the reader to obtain a feel for the wide variety of views expressed, the format of the conference has generally been maintained: formal remarks, panel discussion, and responses to questions.

Even without the particular events of the first three months of 1969, the timing of the conference was significant: A new administration had just begun to feel its way in Washington, and the end of the 1960's was a good time to begin contemplation of the 1970's. And, after all, 1969 was the twentieth anniversary of the founding of the People's Republic in Peking.

Public interest in China had been heightened by several events on the international scene during late 1968 and early 1969. After the election of the Nixon Administration, Peking had requested the resumption of the ambassador-level Sino-American talks in Warsaw, which had been allowed to lapse for a considerable period. (The Cultural Revolution had interfered seriously with the entire working of the Chinese Foreign Ministry and Chinese foreign-policy making in general.) However, in early February, 1969, the Chinese decided not to attend the Warsaw talks scheduled for February 20. Peking's reason for canceling the appointment was Washington's decision in early February to grant asylum to a Chinese diplomat stationed in The Hague. Then, on March 4, Moscow disclosed a clash that marked a new stage in the Sino-Soviet conflict—an armed exchange in the middle of the frozen Ussuri River. Finally, on March 14, the Nixon Administration proposed that the United States deploy an antiballistic missile (ABM) system, which the Administration described initially as a protection against the threat of a nuclear missile attack from China.

Public interest had been aroused by internal developments within China. It was anticipated that the Ninth Congress of the Chinese Communist Party (CCP) would begin soon. In fact, it was convened in April, 1969. There was widespread speculation about what the composition of the new Party organs would be and also about the implications of the new Party Constitution, a preliminary draft of which had been published in the West several months before the Congress.

Against this background, then, more than a score of speakers and some 2,500 participants came together to probe the basic issues and problems of relations between America and China. Some of the speakers put forth programs for immediate action; others called for attitudinal changes; still others felt that America's most meaningful action would be to continue present policies. This volume brings together their varied and illuminating statements of both fact and opinion. All deserve an attentive hearing.

Lois Dougan Tretiak

ACKNOWLEDGMENTS

On behalf of the National Committee, I wish to express our gratitude to the many contributors, individual and corporate, whose donations helped to make possible the national convocation on "The United States and China: The Next Decade." Further, I wish to thank Professors A. Doak Barnett and Edwin O. Reischauer for serving as editors of this publication. Their willingness to undertake so complicated a task, as well as their judicious concern for maintaining the character and spirit of the Convocation, is much appreciated. I should also like to thank Lois Dougan Tretiak for many hours of hard work in handling most efficiently the more onerous problems of organization and technical editing. Then, too, the staff of the National Committee, in particular Martha Goell, should be commended for its work, much of it in off-hours, in proofreading and in coordinating the many details of editing with the thirty-four authors whose statements make up this exploration of the issues involved in United States–China relations in the next decade.

ROBERT A. SCALAPINO, *Chairman, 1966–68, 1969–70*
National Committee on United States–China Relations

INTRODUCTION

The unhappy relationship between the United States and China is not the only major problem America faces today, nor is it even the most immediately pressing. The whole of civilization continues to rest uneasily on a precarious nuclear balance between the United States and the Soviet Union. White-hot passions in the Middle East constantly threaten to burst into the flames of full-scale warfare. In East Asia itself, the urgent need is to bring an early end to the Vietnam War, but to do so in such a way as to avoid new catastrophes for America and the world. It is indeed a perilous passage the United States is attempting between the Scylla of moving too slowly to end the Vietnam War and the Charybdis of ending it in such a way as to destroy the faith of the world in America and to produce in Americans a sullen unconcern for the Asian half of the world. Beyond this, the United States must define for itself a useful and constructive American role in Asia, once it has extricated itself from the Vietnam quagmire. The United States is also entering a period of crisis in its relations with Japan, as that nation, now the third largest economic unit in the world, reconsiders its security arrangements with the United States, which lie at the heart of any American stance in Asia. No one needs to be reminded of the critical domestic problems America faces— problems that make the public increasingly impatient with foreign involvements that seem to draw attention and resources away from domestic needs.

All these problems, both at home and abroad, are for the moment more in the public eye than is the Sino-American relationship. They are on the front burners, while the China problem seems to be on the back burner, not threatening any immediate blow-up and indeed appearing to go on year after year almost without change. One might ask then: Why should there be a national conference on United States–China relations at a time when other problems seem more immediately explosive?

The answer is that this conference is particularly timely just because the China problem remains on the back burner. The best cooking, diplomatic as well as culinary, may not be the fast fry of crisis negotiations but the slow simmer of gradual understanding and mutual adjustments. An informed public can contribute very little to the one process but a great deal to the other. A discussion at this sort of conference of the delicate and complicated balance between negotiations in Paris and action in Vietnam might do more harm than good, but the careful analysis and study of the Sino-American relationship can be enormously beneficial both to the American public and to its leaders, in part just because the crises of the moment have drawn attention away from the great, underlying problems of Sino-American relations.

To change the metaphor, national maladies like personal ones can be either acute or chronic. To concentrate only on acute ills and ignore chronic ones would be to court disaster. It would mean reliance only on the cruel surgery of war rather than on the healing medicine of diplomacy. Chronic problems often lie behind acute symptoms—or at least aggravate them—and they can become dangerously acute at any time. This is particularly true of the China problem.

The Chinese people constitute close to one-fourth of mankind. Deep suspicions and bitter hostility between this fourth of humanity and the third of the world the United States represents in economic terms can only be viewed as a dangerous chronic disease for the whole world. The disease itself holds vast perils for the world, and it seriously complicates the other ills of Asia. Sino-American tension aggravates the whole unhappy Vietnam situation and is the underlying problem in attempting to define a desirable American stance in post-

Vietnam Asia. It feeds the crisis in America's relations with Japan, for most Japanese blame the United States for their own unsatisfactory relationship with China, and many are deeply fearful that the present security treaty they have with the United States may eventually involve Japan in war with China. Even assuming that the present East Asian crises are all successfully surmounted, the China problem will still be there, possibly looming larger than ever, as China develops its nuclear capacities and its other great potentialities. No, the China-America relationship is not a matter that America can afford to forget while attending to more immediately painful ills. It is a cancer in world relations that demands constant and careful attention.

It is high time to start giving this problem the thoughtful attention it requires. Back burner or not, the simmering stew of Sino-American relations needs attention now. Whatever we start to cook will take a long time to finish. Relations between two such massive units as China and the United States move slowly. Peking may at present be in such political disarray as to be unable to react quickly in any case, but perhaps this gives the United States the chance to bring the stew to a state that will prove temptingly aromatic to whatever leadership eventually does emerge there.

EDWIN O. REISCHAUER
Chairman, First National
Convocation, National Committee
on United States–China Relations

I.

Political
Trends
in China—
Today
and Tomorrow

LUCIAN W. PYE

The relationship the United States and China can build up over time depends in large part on the international environment and on China. Although policy is not always based upon fact, it ought at least to start with a deep appreciation of the fundamental facts. In the past, the China policy of the United States particularly has been plagued by a series of myths, illusions, and feelings that conjured up different images of China in American minds. Policy tried to deal with these images, but what is illusion to one man is reality to another. Historically, this has been a constant difficulty and peculiar problem with respect to China, where it is extraordinarily difficult to get at reality.

The Chinese may insist that there cannot be "two Chinas," that there is only one China. Yet, it seems there are as many Chinas as observers of China. Everyone comes away from experiences with China with different impressions; indeed, the foreign policies of the countries of the world toward China reflect a rich variety of pictures of China—almost as though each country were dealing with a different entity.

The position of the Soviet Union is that China has gone mad with emotion, violating the most basic premises of Marxism-Leninism; China is practicing black magic as far as the real ideals of Communism are concerned. To the Soviets, China is one of the more dangerous countries in the world.

The Japanese seem to be dealing with a China that is, in large part, a trading partner but also with a China that they feel is still related to the great Confucian tradition that Japan, too, shares. During the 1950's, the Indians viewed China as benign, a China that reflected and was responsive to the principles of Bandung. More recently, the Indians have seen China as an enemy. The Pakistanis, feeling that any nation willing to fight India cannot be all bad, have developed a new friendly feeling toward China.

The reality that is China begins with its enormous population: 800 million people.[1] Can that many people really be ruled by one government? Not so long ago, the thought of 800 million, maybe closer to a billion, people being ruled by one government was a dream of world government.

Secondly, there is the uniqueness of China that stems from the distinctive qualities of China's history. In a sense, Chinese civilization was the one great alternative civilization to the West. There is here the problem of the meeting of great civilizations and not merely the clash of nation-states. How do we deal with all this? How does China fit into the world? For the last 100 years, all the major powers have had difficulty in coping with this question.

Thirdly, there is the fact of a changing China, of an old China and a new China. What "Communist China" are we talking about? Chinese Communist rule has had a certain quality of vintage years—each year seems to bring a different set of policies. During the first decade, there was a rather orderly approach to affairs, but, more recently, came the con-

---

[1] Estimates of China's current population vary. Different speakers at the convocation used figures varying from 700 million to 800 million.

fusion of the Great Leap Forward and then the Great Proletarian Cultural Revolution.[2]

The problem of comprehending the realities of China lies in China's isolation and the problem of slicing through the mass of Chinese propaganda. Despite these difficulties, it is important to put together different impressions and pieces of evidence to acquire a sense of China that would be useful in terms of American policy. It is the task of this panel to set the stage for positive discussions by trying to outline the main dimensions of current Chinese Communist realities, as seen by each participant.

[2] In an effort to overcome bottlenecks and imbalances in its economy and to catch up with the economically advanced nations, China launched the Great Leap Forward in 1958. Among its major features were the rapid formation of communes (new and larger collectivized organizations), an emphasis on small-scale, local industry (backyard furnaces) as well as heavy industry, and frenzied efforts to meet high production goals. The effort overloaded the transportation network, overtaxed China's manpower and fuel resources, and led to exaggerated production claims. Within about a year, the economy sagged, and China entered a three-year period of food shortages and industrial dislocation. See statements by Alexander Eckstein and Walter Galenson in Chapter 3. This book includes several interpretations of the Cultural Revolution, which began in China in 1965–66. See, for example, the statements of David Oancia, Richard M. Pfeffer, and Roderick MacFarquhar in this chapter.

RICHARD L. WALKER

After twenty years of Communist rule in mainland China, of a divided China in world affairs, of unremitting hostility by the Communist leaders in Peking to what they call "American imperialism," of revolutionary change in China, and of even more revolutionary changes in the rest of the world, it is indeed time for a fresh look at a complex issue, which has been of trouble and concern not only to Washington but to Moscow, New Delhi, and many other capitals of the world. It is increasingly evident that some of the assumptions and utterances that have become clichés over the years must be re-examined. The world is not dealing today with the China that, only a few years ago, it thought it knew.

Two decades ago a seemingly unified Communist leadership came to power with formidable resources at its disposal. Although economic chaos, war-weariness, corruption, lack of national unity, and other problems faced Mao Tse-tung and his fellow Communists in 1949, they were able to draw upon a tremendous reservoir of political resources, which offered them promise of success in moving China into the modern world: they had the support of many Chinese intellectuals and technicians; they were able to evoke vigorous expressions of Chinese nationalism and national pride; they tended to have the support of the newly emergent nations in a period when anticolonialism held sway in the world; and at first they even had some sympathy for their attempt to transform China into a "new China" among those at home and abroad who then sensed the implications of Mao's candid admission: "Yes, my dear gentlemen, we are dictatorial!"

Today, the Communist leaders search in vain for the resources that promised so much for the "new China." It is increasingly clear that mainland China cannot be judged in terms of what seemed a successful experiment during the first decade. Chairman Mao and those who have joined his court of flatterers have squandered the resources that portended success. In fact, the term "new China" is no longer even heard, nor is there an optimism or faith in its progress. Internally, Mao has thrown away the support of one group after another in the population in a manner that has resulted in the "alienation of the intellectuals" (if that phrase might be applied to China), the disillusionment of youth who have been used as pawns in a combination power struggle and mammoth attempt at permanent revolutionary thrust, the breakup of the once monolithic Party, and the imposition of military rule. Externally, Mao has squandered the support of once sympathetic neutralists, of once enthusiastic nationalist leaders in Asia, Africa, and Latin America, and of once solidly committed Communist allies and fraternal Parties.

The obvious and important turning point was the frenzied Great Leap Forward, which began in 1958. Since then, Chairman Mao has increasingly lived in a world of fantasy. Many resources that the Communist leaders could tap in 1949 had already been wasted before the Great Leap. This was abundantly clear during the blooming of the "Hundred Flowers" in 1957, when intellectuals made it clear that they felt their support and faith had been betrayed.[1] The Cultural Revolution, which got under way in 1966, is Mao's most recent revolutionary attempt to stem the tide of a downward trend in morale, support, unity, and even hope for his program. This downward trend separates the pre-Leap first decade from the struggle for "adjustments" of the second decade of Communist rule in China. The Cultural Revolution and its revelations have even brought into question many previous assessments of the first decade of the People's Republic of China.

The totalitarian mode of operation and some of the attitudes attendant upon it have been increasingly frozen as the cult of Mao Tse-tung and of the thought of Mao have grown. The Maoists have found their world inside China and even in the Chinese Communist Party peopled with "demons, freaks, and monsters," and they have exhibited a paranoia similar to that during the late Stalin period in the Soviet Union. While proclaiming that 90 per cent of the people of the world are on their side, they have seen dark plots against them everywhere. They have accused the Soviet Union and the United States of jointly plotting to bring India into a scheme to encircle China. (Moscow, meanwhile, charges Washington and Peking with collusion against the Soviet Union.) The totalitarian mode has been reflected in arbitrary decisions, a fetish for secrecy, and what appears to the outside world to be irrational extremes perhaps best symbolized by the "little red book" containing quotations from Mao Tse-tung—the talisman of the Cultural Revolution—and the proclamation that China's second thermonuclear explosion, in December, 1968, was made

---

[1] During May, 1957, Chinese intellectuals were invited to criticize shortcomings in contemporary Chinese society. After some reluctance, they roundly attacked the regime—and were abruptly stifled in June. This period of criticism, later known as the Hundred Flowers, was sanctioned by Mao Tse-tung in a speech in which he said: "Let a hundred flowers bloom, let a hundred schools of thought contend."

possible by, and was a reflection of, a victory of the thought of Mao Tse-tung.

Mainland China is clearly in disarray. Several changes have occurred that will have a decisive influence on the patterns of approach that various peoples and leaders in the outside world adopt. A few deserve mention.

1. *The fracturing of the top leadership.* Not only has the aging Communist elite been withering away, but the remaining leaders have seen their own unity irreparably fractured. There has been a formidable breakdown in mutual confidence. The Cultural Revolution documentation clearly raises this question: Who trusts whom in China today? The ruling elite is divided, scheming, positioning, and hedging. There is at the present time in China little clear central direction and less immediate prospect for lasting unity at the top.

2. *The Chinese Communist Party has been shattered.* A recent count, for example, shows that of 93 full members of the Eighth Central Committee still alive, 41 have been definitely purged and the whereabouts of 18 others is unknown. Purges of equal proportions have been carried down to the provincial levels and below and throughout the entire structure of government. The Ninth Congress of the Chinese Communist Party, in April, 1969, could hardly have been expected to do more than paper over the damage.

3. *The fall of Chairman Mao.* Despite the current flurry of activity in support of Mao and his thought, it is becoming increasingly clear that his fellow leaders have for some time lost faith in his ability to answer the needs and problems of China. There is a formidable credibility gap in China today centering on an overly romanticized figure who has proven himself, though brilliant and masterful in some fields, supremely ignorant of the outside world and of the forces that make for economic development and political modernization. As Professor James T. Myers has pointed out in his study of

the Mao cult,[2] the "fall" of the "great helmsman" really began with the Great Leap.

4. *Growth in power of the regional military leaders and the forces of regionalism.* It is no longer even clear that the central military leadership can exercise complete authority over strategic military forces under the control of the great military area commanders. Some regional military leaders have been exhibiting tendencies toward local autonomy.

5. *The breakdown of lines of authority during the present state of flux.* For the outside world a number of questions have to be answered before any sort of dialogue with China should be initiated: Whom does one contact? With whom does one deal? Who is running foreign policy and for how long? At present, it is even necessary for one to ask whether there is any real meaning to statements suggesting that "Peking wants" this or that or "China will react" in one manner or another.

It has become increasingly evident that the myth of the "new China" has been confronting some of the persistent realities of the "old China." One of these realities is the tremendous population in mainland China. Is it possible that there are too many energetic, intelligent, sophisticated, ambitious Chinese people to be governed from a single political center? Political scientists have not really confronted the question of whether a population can reach a point beyond which traditional political institutions, or even modern ones, will cease to function adequately. Can 800 million people be effectively governed under a unitary political system?

There are other old realities that have become more prominent as faith in the Maoist approach has faltered: provincial ties and loyalties, national minorities, agrarian production and relations, political succession and stability, and even the matter

[2] James T. Myers, "The Fall of Chairman Mao," *Current Scene* (Hong Kong), Vol. 6, No. 10 (June 15, 1968).

of the Chinese written language and the thought patterns it imposes.

Two decades of Communist rule in China have made it increasingly clear that the Communists as well as the outside world have been dealing with a civilization and not a nation. For more than a century and a quarter, one of the most profound and rich civilizations mankind has ever developed has been attempting to adjust to a world where the science, technology, and rationality developed in the West seem destined to hold sway. Sensitive about the manner in which the Japanese adapted to the scientific West, prideful in their own sense of historic destiny, Chinese leaders in this century have sought solutions to a problem that is more cultural than political.

For the past two decades, a supremely self-confident and romantic utopian has attempted by a mass-line strategy to lead his people into the world of the third quarter of the twentieth century. Obviously, changes have been made, and it is certain that Chinese civilization has been altered in many areas. But what Mao has failed to learn, although the years have been demonstrating it clearly, is that cultural patterns usually change at a glacial tempo and that Chinese civilization has been his formidable enemy.

The problem of bringing China's traditional agrarian society into the mainstream of today's world has not been solved by the techniques of collectivization, mass mobilization, mass mesmerism, and purges. In these terms some of the patterns of Chinese adjustment to the world of the space age may have a significance beyond the immediate political disparities in size and influence. For this reason, some aspects of America's China policy may have been more successful than its frequent critics suspect. We may have waited with Oriental-like patience while the Maoist model proved itself an inadequate answer. As we look to the future, we know that the problem remains that of a civilization's accommodating itself to the rest of the world. The process of adjustment is not likely to be easy or painless—for the Chinese or for the rest of the world. We may therefore be more realistic if we try to understand the process in cultural terms and stop searching for a Western political formula as an easy or quick solution.

DAVID OANCIA

As a result of the Cultural Revolution, which began in 1966, the People's Liberation Army (PLA) [1] has emerged as the dominant and the major cohesive force in China. This means that the people who ran the Communist Party have been neutralized, that the "experts" and professionals have been purged or relegated to secondary positions, and that the architects of the upheaval have had to turn increasingly to disciplined armed forces officers and men for help in containing the centrifugal forces they set free. China and its people have paid an incredibly high price, a price that most of us on this continent would consider exorbitant, as a result of Mao's Promethean urge to refashion in his own image the individuals making up his nation and to establish a policy his successors would be obligated to follow for at least another generation.

When I arrived in China in the autumn of 1965, no one

---

[1] The term includes the army, navy, and air force.

was talking very much about a cultural revolution. Stores displayed an impressive array of consumer goods, shopping areas were being given a face-lift, and great emphasis was being placed on improving the quality and increasing the quantity of the goods produced by the country's factories and farms. People were trying to enjoy the new affluence that followed the era of shortages and hardships, which they associated with the Great Leap Forward.

A number of political campaigns were under way, but people generally did not seem to pay much attention to them. One of these was intended to improve traffic safety by knocking some sense into the heads of cyclists who did not bother to stick to their lanes on the sides of the broad boulevards or to use their lights at night. For about a month, the police spent an extraordinary amount of time lecturing cyclists who erred. The offenders would listen dutifully to the lecture and would promise to improve their habits. Then, while the officer watched, they carefully observed the rules as they rode off. They did this for about ten yards or so. When they felt they were beyond the officer's clutches, they flicked off their lights and swung to the center of the street, where the traffic was not as heavy.

In 1965, I visited several farm communes and industrial plants. The people with whom I spoke emphasized the efforts they were making to improve quality and increase production. They were preoccupied with problems that confront any manager, and they paid only the scantiest lip service to the thoughts of Mao and to political campaigns. Within six months, however, there was to be a dramatic change. Everyone then tried to demonstrate his political activism, his eagerness to study Mao's writings, and the dedication to apply the lessons learned in his own operations.

Nevertheless, there was an undercurrent of anxiety. The people feared that the escalation of the Vietnam War would engulf them and that China would be drawn into a shooting conflict with the United States. A vicious debate raged in the ranks of the top leadership over what China's response should be if this came to pass. The military professionals argued that the leadership should put the nation on a war footing and prepare to counter the threat close to the southern frontier. The fundamentalists—Mao and his deputy, Defense Minister Lin Piao—argued that guerrilla warfare should be used to counter the threat. This conflict was to erupt later into what is called the Cultural Revolution.

The storm clouds of the Cultural Revolution began to be evident early in 1966. The army's political department convened a big conference (which Lo Jui-ch'ing, then the army chief of staff, did not attend) and decreed that Mao's thought was to guide the operations of the armed forces. By April and May, the army newspaper and army spokesmen were leading the drive against the "professionals" in the armed forces ranks and the pragmatists in the civilian leadership. In May, 1966, some students began to move.

I visited the College of Iron and Steel Technology in late May. It had a modern plant with excellent library facilities and books from all over the world, including the United States, but no one was listening to lectures or using the library. Instead, the students were active on the campuses using loud-speakers in demonstrations to show their determination to fight the "power-holders" whom Mao said were taking the capitalist road.

In June, 1966, the storm broke. The leaders of the Peking Municipal Communist Party Committee, the army chief of staff, and leading propagandists were purged, and the Party sought to involve as many people as possible in support of this move. There were demonstrations from sunrise until 3:00 A.M. Thousands of people marched under banners and chanted slogans wishing Mao long life and supporting the decision to "reorganize" the Peking Party Committee. Within a couple of weeks, schools closed, universities were shut, and violent conflicts were taking place on the campuses. Young people were organized to attack their teachers and the political backers of these teachers. The response of the people who were under attack was often predictable; rather than face the attacks, they attempted suicide. The young people who were leading this movement—the Red Guards—were Mao's troops in his drive against the old culture and old habits.

In mid-August, the attacks were intensified. Young people involved were at first uncertain about how to behave. They were "helped" by activists in their thirties or forties who stayed in the background and egged on the students and told them how to proceed. There was much violence, which those of us on the outside considered senseless and cruel.

A Catholic church and a Protestant chapel in Peking were sacked; crosses, crucifixes, and statues were taken down and smashed, and busts of Mao were put up in their place. A Muslim mosque in the southwestern part of the city was sacked, and the Muslim religious leaders who ran from it were assaulted. One of these people, prostrate on the street, was kicked and beaten by the young Red Guards. This was labeled a drive against the old custom of religion.

Within about three or four weeks, the youngsters had begun to fan out through the countryside, spreading the pattern developed in Peking. They ransacked homes and took away books, heirlooms, and *objets d'art* to Red Guard warehouses. This was at the beginning of the attack on the Party organization. However, this phase was not fully successful because Party officials at various levels organized their own supporters to counter the young activists from Peking.

By the end of the year, conflict had intensified. The leaders of the Cultural Revolution—including Mao's wife, Chiang Ch'ing, his former political secretary, Ch'en Po-ta, and K'ang Sheng, an expert on intelligence and security matters and in dealing with other Communist governments—decided that the time had come to authorize the young Red Guards to capture the people whom Mao considered to be "capitalist-roaders." The wife of the President of China,[2] Mme. Liu Shao-ch'i (Wang Kuang-mei), was tricked into going out to one of the universities in early 1967 by a phone call telling her her daughter had been injured. There she was subjected to a criticism and struggle meeting. Furthermore, the former Mayor of Peking, P'eng Chen, the former army chief of staff, Lo Jui-ch'ing, the former propaganda chief, Lu Ting-i, and a member of the Party Secretariat accused of planting listening devices to keep those branded as capitalist-roaders posted on what Mao was doing were captured and taken before huge crowds and forced to listen to charges leveled by young people who did not always know the truth.

I can remember some of the photographs that were being posted on the wall at that time. One showed Lo Jui-ch'ing with his leg in a cast, forced to sit with his head bowed, his arm being twisted behind his back by a young soldier while young activists harangued him with charges of plotting to usurp the power of the army.

By early 1967, the army was ordered to play a more active role to help the Red Guards and the revolutionary rebels seize power from the bureaucratic Party personnel. I was talking to the director of a fertilizer factory when an army unit arrived. He did not know what the army was going to do, but he did not think they would try to run his operation because, in his estimation, the soldiers lacked the technical skill.

---

[2] The former President of China, Liu Shao-ch'i, was the highest-placed target of the Cultural Revolution and an early victim of it. What appeared to have been long-standing differences between Mao and Liu resulted in Liu's being named the "number one Party person in authority taking the capitalist road" and his being charged with every manner of ideological crime and a number of personal moral failings as well.

Later, when the time came for me to leave China, I had two experiences that illustrate some of the problems one is likely to meet in trying to deal with China at the present time. My Chinese friends arranged an amiable dinner at which we ate Peking duck and drank *mao-t'ai*[3] and brandy. I raised with them the question of whether they thought it would be possible for Canada and China to improve their relations to a point where an exchange of diplomatic missions would be possible. They worked for an official government agency, and they were well informed. Their answer was friendly and unequivocal. China was prepared to establish diplomatic relations with Canada on the principles enunciated by Chairman Mao in 1949—on the basis of equality, mutual benefit, and mutual respect for territorial integrity and sovereignty.

When I was leaving, I was shown another face of China. The customs and security officials represented a force in the Chinese administration that any nation will have to consider in a quest to improve relations and extend contacts with the government of the most populous nation on earth. The customs and security men were not interested in making a good impression. They went through everything I had looking for any "state secrets" I might wittingly or unwittingly be trying to smuggle out of their country. They went to incredible lengths. They riffled through books, read all personal documents and correspondence, and seized many books and papers. In their quest, they ripped the insoles out of my wife's shoes, pulled the lining out of baggage and hand bags, and took apart mounted pictures to see if anything was concealed in them. Finally, after two different sessions of this, I was at last allowed to leave. It was not a happy departure.

I think that anyone who tries to deal with China in the future will have to determine whom he will have to deal with.

[3] A fiercely strong, clear alcoholic beverage distilled primarily in Kweichow Province, in Southwest China.

Will it be the Chinese who are still suspicious and antagonistic to the outside world and its representatives? Or, hopefully, will it be those who are correct and friendly and who show a real interest in expanding their nation's contacts and relations according to the principles laid down by Mao almost twenty years ago?

RICHARD M. PFEFFER

I wish to make several points, which seem to me fundamental, concerning the nature of this convocation. While my points are not limited in scope to the substance of this particular panel, I raise them now both because this is the initial session and because there appears to be no more appropriate time to do so.

First, I believe that the structure of this convocation is so asymmetrical that the very purpose of the effort—to raise our understanding of Sino-American relations—is subverted by the manner in which the panels have been organized. Let me make this point clear by means of a hypothetical case. Suppose that today in Peking a conference entitled "China and the United States: The Next Decade" is being held and that that conference is divided into four main panels: the first panel being "Political Trends in the United States—Today and Tomorrow"; the second, "The United States and World Security"; the third, "United States' Development, Trade, and the World Economy"; and the fourth, "China and the United States—

Policy Options for the Future." What would we realistically expect from a conference so structured? Insight into the *relationship between* China and the United States? Balance? Objectivity?

Or, alternatively, let us suppose that we learned of a conference in Peking dealing with Sino-Soviet relations, in which every panel dealt exclusively with the Soviet Union, save the final one, which dealt with China's policy alternatives vis-à-vis the Soviet Union. Or suppose the subject was Peru and Chile, and the configuration remained the same. What would we expect? I submit that we would be skeptical about any conference so structured. We would reasonably assume that any serious conference concerning relations between two countries should examine the attitudes, internal dynamics, and foreign-policy patterns of *both* of the relevant countries. To study only one of the parties to a relationship, when the goal is to understand the relationship, indicates intellectual shallowness or cultural blindness.

The asymmetry of this convocation, to my mind, means that, however good our individual sessions on China may be, the convocation is unlikely to produce objective analysis of relations between the United States and China. Given our nearly exclusive concern with China, it would have been more candid to have called the convocation "Our China Problem." Examining the future of Sino-American relations without dealing with the American component is, to put the matter in the simplistic, mechanical figures of speech to which we have all become so accustomed, too much like hypothesizing about the resultant vector of one billiard ball that is about to be struck by another, without studying the relevant facts about the striking ball. One cannot know which way ball one will move when struck without first having information about ball two. It is the element of interaction that constitutes the core of what we normally mean when we speak of relationships, be they mechanical, political, or personal.

But why, I ask myself, has this convocation deviated from the sensible symmetry of structure we might expect. I have no certain answers to that question. I need not, nor do I necessarily, attribute the deviation to bad faith. Unconscious attitudes may well have been determinative. Nevertheless, the issue remains: Why has this convocation been structured so one-sidedly? And that issue cannot be resolved by the reply that there was no intention to so bias the discussion. Moreover, the biases built into the structure of this conference are not random. They reflect the biases of the liberal approach to Sino-American relations, so dominant in academic, business, and government circles today. And, of course, that is not surprising, since the prime movers of this first national convocation largely represent the liberal establishment that is responsible for America's China policy. Consequently, if we can understand why the convocation is biased, we may perhaps gain some understanding of the American component in the relationship and thereby shed additional light on the quality of that relationship.

Perhaps the conference organizers felt that there was insufficient time to examine both the United States and China. But, then, why did they choose to examine the Chinese component rather than the American one? They may have believed it to be more important for the understanding of Sino-American relations to study China than to study America. I do not agree. And I question again the validity of the notion that, in examining a relationship, one can usefully deal with one of the parties and not the other. Do we really believe that domestic developments in the United States and American foreign policy in general are not factors influencing China? And, more than that, can we believe that these factors do not affect relations between China and the United States, if only through their impact on America's China policy? Such a belief would be patently absurd.

Or relatedly, perhaps the organizers of the convocation

thought our understanding of the United States was already adequate—that it is China rather than the United States that demands our attention. But I would have thought that events of recent years would have disabused us of such complacent, self-righteous visions. If we look to our ghettos, to our universities, to our own political conventions, and to Vietnam, surely we must recognize that we are only beginning to understand ourselves. How much more difficult it must be for China to understand us.

Or perhaps we feel more comfortable and less presumptuous speaking in sweeping terms of China—of its past, its present, and its future—than we do speaking so simplistically about the United States, which daily confronts us in all its complexity. It does, after all, at least require more gall to apply to America and before an American audience the kind of vague, holistic analysis we less judiciously apply to China. Again, we fool ourselves if we think that our relative ignorance of China in any way justifies treating it as if it were less complex than the United States.

Beyond this first point regarding the convocation's asymmetry I would like to make a broader point concerning the significance of conferences of this sort, however they may be structured. I would like to enter a plea for modesty. We do not systematically understand very much in this world, either as journalists, as social scientists, as businessmen, as policymakers, or as concerned citizens. Aside from the ideologues of the left and right, who would have predicted ten years ago that the United States would be fighting an obscene land war in Asia in support of a puppet government? Who predicted the violent polarization that has occurred in the United States between races and generations? Who predicted in 1960 or 1962 that Richard Nixon would be President of the United States in 1969? And if we pass over the failures of prediction— I do not assume prediction to be the only standard for validity —who can say that we really understand what is happening in our own foreign policy and domestically in the United States? I suggest, once more, that we have barely taken the first step in acquiring that kind of systematic self-knowledge.

If we do not succeed in understanding ourselves, can we understand China—a country concerning which our cultural and political biases, compounded by our anxieties and igno-rance, have produced stupid policy and, too frequently, poor journalism and mediocre scholarship? It is no exaggeration to say that we have anticipated few of the major events in China over the last twenty years. And the after-the-fact rationaliza-tions and "explanations" of these events are so contradictory that it frequently remains problematical which is correct and how much any help us to understand China. Which is to say that expert opinion—particularly on China—must be taken with a large grain of salt. Our generalizations at best are tenta-tive. We make educated guesses, even while we pretend to more.

Now, after that none-too-brief introduction, it is my turn to "pretend to more." The Cultural Revolution, to my mind, is one of the most important events of twentieth-century China, a very significant event in the history of comparative Communism (if that term still retains any essential meaning), and, perhaps, even one of the more significant social move-ments of world history. The Cultural Revolution is not a simple or a single phenomenon. It was not, like Pallas Athena, created full-grown from a god's brow. Various groupings within the elite, the masses, and the middle levels of power in China, for their own reasons, are involved in the Cultural Revolution. And the interpretations of the Cultural Revolution, tending to focus on one or more of its components, differ widely. Some analyses take it primarily as a personal power struggle; some, as an institutional struggle between Party and army; and others, as a bigger and better Maoist purge. Some see the Cul-tural Revolution as wholly irrational, an example of Mao's putative megalomania; some, as a quasi-religious search for ultimate value; some, as a conflict between ideology and organization; some, as a response to America's Vietnam policy; some, as the expression of xenophobic, juvenile delinquents. Others conceive of the Cultural Revolution as an attack by the "outs" of Chinese society upon the "ins," as an attack on privilege and bureaucracy. There is some truth and much overlapping in all these interpretations.

The Cultural Revolution, like all substantial revolutions, is so complex a series of events that it is difficult to encompass its meanings and levels of reality within any single analytic framework. One analyst suggests, derisively, that the Cultural Revolution is "an enigmatic multiple power struggle, wrapped in a crusade, and superimposed on a scattering of more or less spontaneous, more or less politicized student riots, strikes, peasant uprisings, mutinies, and palace coups." Melodrama and biases aside, this description at least indicates the variety of events and groups involved in the Cultural Revolution and suggests that the relationship between it and the phenomena we know holistically as the Cultural Revolution is problematic.

In the time remaining, I want to examine one component of the Cultural Revolution: Mao's goals. Such a focus, while useful to narrow the scope of concern, is not without its own difficulties. In the first place, Mao obviously did not have an advance blueprint to guide him along the sinuous course of the Cultural Revolution. Mao is neither superman nor god. Second, in trying to extrapolate what Mao intended from actual events, one is faced with the problem of distinguishing results from intentions and words. Mao acted within the context of particular power configurations, and one cannot facilely assume that what happened reasonably reflects Mao's goals. Moreover, to further complicate matters, the power configurations during the Cultural Revolution have been somewhat fluid, changing in part in response to the intensity of Maoist attacks and opposition resistance. In short, Mao is no puppeteer, pulling strings to animate the Cultural Revolution. He can neither achieve all that he might like, nor can he anticipate in advance many consequences of his acts.

Nevertheless, based on Mao's greatness as a leader, his values, and his historical experience, it is difficult to believe that he did not have some vision of what he sought to accomplish within the apparent exigencies of the power context. To fail to attribute that sort of vision to Mao is to trivialize the man and the entire Cultural Revolution. Moreover, if the Cultural Revolution has shown us one thing, it is the stupendous power of the supreme leader and of ideology, which he can shape through propaganda to meet his needs.

It seems likely that Mao had many goals when he unleashed the Cultural Revolution, some minimal, others maximal. While I do not wish to slight the minimal goals—such as Mao's desire to purge particular individuals and, in the fashion of past, less intense campaigns to shake up the bureaucracies of China—I focus here on Mao's maximal goals largely because the intensity and scope of the Cultural Revolution seem unintelligible without considering them. Mao's maximal goals may include training a successor generation in revolution by encouraging youth to wage revolution from below (that is, without the disciplined control from above exercised in intra-Party purges), reinstating in practice the revolutionary ideals of equality and mass participation, and, relatedly, transforming the nature of bureaucracy by establishing *counter-institutions*.

Let me be more concrete. One can see Mao's development, at least since the Great Leap Forward in 1958, in terms of his increasing rejection of elements of Marxism-Leninism and his increasing concern for the styles and goals expressed by Rousseau and the early Marx. Marxism-Leninism embodies the central belief that technological progress in history produces the preconditions for the good society. The belief that industrialization will produce proletarianization to a significant degree justifies withholding moral judgment while working to achieve the industrialized society. China's revolutionary leaders' shared belief in this fusion of morality and technology through history enabled them to preserve their consensus with the faith that their different goals—for example, modernization, national power, a society of virtuous men—ultimately were compatible. This consensus increasingly broke down after the Great Leap: China's "organization men" focused on such goals as modernization and organizational regularity, and Mao became increasingly skeptical that modernization would lead to the good society. He came to pursue certain elements of Chinese Communist ideology—the moral ones—at the expense of the others—the technological ones. In short, Mao in the 1960's was no longer willing to withhold moral judgment on China's course in the 1960's and 1970's.

Mao became increasingly aware that the Chinese revolution had produced a rather inflexible bureaucracy and a privileged elite devoted to suppressing the Maoist components of the revolution in favor of more pragmatic modernizing goals and methods. In this light, the Cultural Revolution appears to be Mao's attempt to restore the historic balance among the components of the Chinese revolution and, even more difficult, to institutionalize in counter-institutions Mao's own moral concerns. The goal of institutionalizing revolution, of creating permanent revolution, may not be achievable. To achieve it, Mao has attempted to set leader above Party, to elevate his thought above Party and above any alternative ideology on which the Party might rely in opposition to Maoist values and standards of legitimacy, and to re-institutionalize the role of the masses as "participants" in the on-going Chinese revolution. Mao has done all this in order to institutionalize forces to counteract those bureaucratic and inegalitarian tendencies that will reassert themselves when Chinese society is again normalized.

The recently reported new Party Constitution reflects this attempt. In it, the leader is glorified; the Party, save in conjunction with the leader, is described less gloriously than heretofore; Mao's thought is taken as the embodiment and highest form of Marxism-Leninism today; Lin Piao, apparently one of Mao's stanchest supporters in recent years, is named successor to Mao as Party Chairman, thereby excluding the Central Committee from the decision; and the Chinese Communist Party is explicitly required to listen to the masses outside the Party and to be supervised by them. The attempt, as suggested, is to institutionalize a kind of permanent revolution by building tension into the system.

The attempt is so radical that it may appear to us to be doomed to inevitable failure. The relatively conservative influence of the People's Liberation Army, so apparent in recent months, more specifically suggests that Mao's goals are unlikely to be achieved in the foreseeable future. Whether the Cultural Revolution will emerge again in the future remains to be seen. But, in any event, Mao has tried through politics and in history to transform a society in a manner that political theorists like Rousseau only wrote about. Where Rousseau wrote of the messiah-like great leader who comes to earth once and charismatically transforms the society and sets up enduring institutions, Mao—for better or worse—has tried to play the role of that great leader. He has attempted to transform Chinese society. And he has tried to ensure, to the extent possible, that the revolution he has initiated will be perpetuated.

Only time will tell whether Mao has been at least minimally successful and, if so, what that success will mean for China and for the world.

RODERICK MacFARQUHAR

Professor Pfeffer has done a major service in his remarks. He has attempted to look at the Cultural Revolution from the point of view of Mao Tse-tung himself, to whom I would also attribute the major role in launching this incredible movement. I would like to add one major point to the analysis: the role of the Sino-Soviet dispute in the launching of the Cultural Revolution.

It should be constantly reiterated that Mao Tse-tung was born at a time of Chinese disruption and humiliation at the hands of foreign imperial powers. Mao Tse-tung and all his generation, whether they are now on the mainland or not, wanted above all to end that humiliation and to create a strong and unified China. One of the major reasons why Mao embraced Communism was that he saw in Leninism a doctrine and in the Soviet Union under Lenin a country and a leader opposed to imperialism.

In the late 1950's and early 1960's, however, Mao felt that the Soviet Union, for long the leading element in the struggle against imperialism, was defecting from that struggle, that the Soviet Union was prepared to have dealings with the United States. The Soviet Union, moreover, seemed prepared to sacrifice Communist China's goals in the interest of those dealings.

At this stage, he began to examine what had gone wrong in Russia in order to explain the defection of the Soviet Union from the anti-imperialist crusade. When he had made his examination, he decided that the real cause was the loss of militancy on the part of the Communist Party and its leaders. In the early 1960's, Mao's abiding concern became an attempt to re-create revolutionary militancy within China and, above all, to ensure that the people who succeeded him and his colleagues would be men like himself, with the same utopian grand vision of society.

Appalled at the decline of Soviet militancy in international affairs, Mao had a vision of Communism crumbling throughout the world under the onslaught of the "sugar coated bullets" of material prosperity. It must have been a traumatic experience for a man who had witnessed the disintegration of traditional Chinese civilization to realize that the new one he had fought to introduce in its place might go the same way. For, by the early 1960's, most of his colleagues apparently believed that the Party's prime aim must be to concentrate on economic development, even at the expense of revolutionary militancy.

Mao came to view the Party bureaucracy as a routinized instrument of administration and repression, which stifled the idealism and spontaneity of the masses. Thus it had to be purged. He saw the educational system and the style of economic management geared to expertise. The former created a new class of intellectuals, administrators, and managers divorced from and superior to the workers and peasants; the latter suppressed the inventiveness of the masses. Thus both had to be radically reformed. If all this led to civil strife, that would have to be endured, for China had to be preserved as the bastion of world revolution.

Probably Mao underestimated the amount of turmoil that would ensue when he unleashed the Red Guards to topple the Party bureaucracy. He may not have foreseen that his young supporters would split into bitterly opposed factions, often fighting each other to the death. But actually the record shows that Mao has always distrusted intellectuals (and, in Chinese terms, the young students are intellectuals). He has always maintained that, although the youth can provide the spark to light the prairie fire of revolution in modern China, only the assumption of leadership by the working class can ensure that the revolution will persist and win victory.

The brutal curbing of the Red Guards may owe much to the fury of the local military commanders who are now effectively responsible for law and order in China. But the official transfer of the banner of revolutionary leadership to the workers is pure Mao. He could reasonably calculate that, even if the ardor of these Red Guards was thoroughly squashed by this transfer of leadership, this would not deter future generations of Red Guards.

But there are more fundamental problems that must trouble Mao. Has he merely substituted a military bureaucracy for a civilian one, with the danger that, after his death, China will not be a revolutionary utopia but a military dictatorship? The danger is increased because the only real constituency of Mao's designated successor, Defense Minister Lin Piao, is the army.

Assuming that Mao remains vigorous for another few years, having succeeded in destroying the Party, he could also reorganize the Party to take over from the army. In the first instance, he would have to try to ensure that the top leadership remained weighted in favor of his Cultural Revolution group and that the second echelon posts were held largely by civilians, however inexperienced. Thereafter, he could try shifting regional commanders away from their local power bases and promote impatient junior officers of the same generation as the new Party officials.

If Mao were to pass from the scene in the near future, none of his successors currently in view would seem to combine the talent, will, and power necessary to restore the élan and prestige of the Party. A Bonapartist regime would then be a real possibility, and Mao's hopes of generations of revolutionary successors would be virtually unrealizable.

There is an even deeper problem. Mao is grappling with what many of the younger generation in the West see as the crucial issue of our time. Can man attain the full development of his personality in an atomized, bureaucratized, industrialized state? Mao is a complex man who sees the importance of organization and leadership but one whose deepest urges seem to be in favor of spontaneity, initiative, and egalitarianism. He has destroyed China's ruling bureaucracy, but he is creating it anew. If he succeeds, will the new Party not degenerate too? He has foreseen this possibility. Thus the Chinese press talks in terms of the need for a second, a third, indeed, an endless Cultural Revolution.

After Mao, will there be another man with the charisma and the self-confidence needed to launch a Cultural Revolution? And will China's 750 million relatively poor people make continual revolution if it means further postponement of economic betterment? Mao hopes the answer will be yes, especially if his teachings are continually drummed into everyone. And he knows that for decades, perhaps centuries to come, a new Mao could still tap the immense reservoir of frustration that exists in China and all other underdeveloped countries— the frustration of an expanding younger generation that can be provided with the education to develop ambitions but not the jobs to satisfy them, a younger generation that sees a new world but realizes it will never grasp it.

Men of law and order are on the rise in China at the moment. But underneath, even if Mao died tomorrow, there will still be ferment. It would be very rash to predict that even a military dictatorship would be able to keep it under control.

PAUL H. KREISBERG

The problems created by confusion, disruption, and conflict inside China have made it very difficult for the Chinese to decide how to pursue either their internal policies or their external policies. Foreign policy, always difficult to conduct, was once seen as being much more difficult for a democratic country to execute than for a totalitarian country because, in a democracy, there were so many more openly conflicting forces at work. The Soviet Union and China had a much easier job than the United States did, so it was thought, because each of them spoke with a unified voice. One always knew what their policy was, and they were able to pursue their policy with a single-minded dedication.

Over the last ten or fifteen years, it has become increasingly clear that Communist countries have exactly the same problems that we do. In fact, they have more problems, because the differences between the various objectives they try to pursue are so dramatically sharp. We have to resolve conflicts between the positions of various groups, between rival views of our relationships with another country or countries, between disagreements about the effect of our action toward one country upon another country, and we have to learn how to balance all these considerations against one another.

These are constant dilemmas for the United States, but they are even more difficult for the Chinese to resolve, since they are faced with a more intense sense of the contradictions between pursuing a national foreign policy and a revolutionary foreign policy, between focusing on ideological and nationalistic objectives. There was a period during which they were able to achieve some reconciliation between the two, but increasingly over the last ten years—and especially since the Cultural Revolution—Peking's national objectives and its revolutionary objectives have come into such intense conflict that almost all policy movement has halted.

Communist China's activities, both internal and external, have been extremely difficult to predict. Few of the key developments that have taken place in the last ten or fifteen years have been fully anticipated by anyone inside or outside the government of the United States—or in any other country that I am aware of. This is related to China's superimposing of ideological policy on top of random activity, individual initiative, and formal bureaucratic planning—which has made it very difficult to see in what direction conflicting forces are going to take Chinese society. This has made China a difficult country with which to negotiate or to have relations—or even not to have relations.

For example, the Chinese have clearly not made up their minds whether it is in their interests to participate in international organizations—not only broad international groups, but international Communist organizations or even Afro-Asian ones. They have found it extremely difficult to decide how much reliance they want to put upon the whole international state system, upon the system of international law, and upon the conventional modes of diplomatic and consular behavior.

When it is in their interests, they use the traditions and language of international law; when it is not, they ignore them. In this respect, they are not all that different from other countries. But the intensity of the conflict in China over what kind of policy they really want to pursue is so great that they have swung far more sharply and dramatically to extremes than most other countries do.

The Chinese inability to decide whether their primary emphasis should be on improving bilateral relations with other countries or on encouraging revolutionary movements inside these countries emerged clearly during Prime Minister Chou En-lai's trip to Africa in April–June, 1965. On the one hand, Chou felt compelled to talk about the need for revolution and the fact that a broad revolution was going to sweep over Africa. On the other hand, he found that this attitude adversely affected China's relations with a number of the African states he did visit and with others he did not visit, including several that specifically canceled outstanding invitations to him.

The Chinese found it difficult to decide, even in terms of their own specific national and economic interest, whether it was more important to maintain a focus on ideological principles in dealing with the Soviet Union and risk the dramatic worsening of Sino-Soviet relations we have seen during the last seven or eight years or to compromise because of China's need for foreign capital, technology, and foreign assistance. They made one decision ten years ago; they could well make a contrary one in the future.

On September 29, 1965, Chinese Foreign Minister Ch'en I, in an open address to journalists in Peking, said that he knew perfectly well that if the Chinese Government were to trade with the United States, this would be in many respects in the interests of China. But he then added that Peking had decided that such a policy would betray the world revolution and reopen China to the "imperialists" and to American "colonial occupation."

Such questions, of course, are similar to those all countries confront at various times. The United States must consider to what extent the values of democracy should supersede or be superimposed upon the need for security or the requirements of specific bilateral state relations or the maintenance of traditional relationships with existing governments. All countries make compromises. To the extent that one can conduct a foreign policy, one has to be able to come to a relatively clear compromise, determining where the balance lies among one's conflicting interests; when the pressures and conflicts generated by one's internal problems, world view, and national interests become too intense, one can no longer conduct a foreign policy. In recent years, this has appeared to be particularly applicable to Communist China.

DISCUSSION

PYE: How is China being ruled? What has happened to the Communist Party apparatus that was built up so carefully over all these years? And what does it mean when we say the military are now ruling? How temporary or permanent is this development?

OANCIA: The PLA as a unified whole has not taken over from the experts, but military personnel are filling the functions that were formerly filled by technocrats, senior bureaucrats, and people at the cabinet-minister level.

The Party organization inside the armed forces did not suffer as much destruction during the Cultural Revolution as did the regular Party apparatus. The Party within the PLA is controlled by the army's general political department and has considerable influence in the country. It is difficult to say whether this will be a permanent feature. The army did relinquish its power in the early 1950's after the civil war, whereupon a civil bureaucracy and Party apparatus were developed.

MAC FARQUHAR: A few of the old Party officials in the provinces and some at the center have been preserved, partly because of loyalty to Mao, partly because they have some bargaining power or a power base that Mao needs, partly because they have switched to his side during the Cultural Revolution. But the provinces are now controlled extremely loosely from Peking. An instructive example gleaned from Red Guard documents of the Cultural Revolution is the instance in which it was impossible for the center to stop two rival feuding Red Guard groups from holding up arms shipments to Vietnam. Finally, Premier Chou En-lai had to call the two groups to Peking. Instead of giving orders, he had to cajole, bully, and persuade. Perhaps the threat of force was in the background, but even that was slightly mitigated. The army was split in that province, too. In the provinces, the norm seems to be control by the local military commander. He is almost always in a very strong position in the new organs of local power known as revolutionary committees.[1]

The regional commanders have a fair degree of autonomy in the local areas. We must remember that these are men who fought against warlordism, who fought to reunite China. I do not believe that any one of them would want to set himself up as an independent warlord. What they want primarily is law and order, ultimately policing with their own troops.

The strength of Mao's position lies in the fact that the central military organization has been purged repeatedly by him. The army does not talk as a body, but his designated successor, Lin Piao, is still able to command a great deal of loyalty, I believe, from the regional commanders individually.

[1] Between early 1967 and September, 1968, revolutionary committees consisting of representatives of the PLA, pro-Mao members of the former Party bureaucracy, and, to a lesser extent, Red Guard leaders were set up in every province, with responsibility for civil administration and the maintenance of law and order. According to the Chinese press, "All affairs, both great and small, are referred to the military representatives sitting as senior members of the revolutionary committees."

WALKER: We should not leave the impression of unity in the PLA. The military forces are very divided and it is really questionable in a number of cases to what extent Lin Piao himself can command and make his command heard in some of the regional military areas. A recent study shows that the average tenure of six of these very formidable regional military leaders has been more than thirteen years. Huang Yung-sheng, who has commanded the Canton military region for almost eighteen years, is now chief of staff of the armed forces, too.

Regional military commanders such as Hsü Shih-yu, Yang Te-chih, and others feel that they know the problems in their own regions and how they can best be solved, so that there is a fair amount of tension and division between the central command and the military regions. Indeed, there has been actual fighting within the PLA. If we are going to talk about the problem of a military takeover, we must understand that there are long-range, long-lasting tensions within the PLA.

QUESTION: [2] To what extent is the Great Leap Forward responsible for the development of the Cultural Revolution?

OANCIA: I think that you have to go back to the Great Leap Forward to find the origins of the Cultural Revolution. I do not think that Mao Tse-tung ever really accepted the idea that the Great Leap was a failure. But the people who had to pick up the pieces, the administrative experts, the technical experts, and the pragmatic leaders, allowed a considerable retreat from the policies that guided the Great Leap. While they picked up the pieces, there was a period of relaxation in which literary people and intellectuals unfolded a campaign vilifying and mocking the father of the Chinese revolution—a situation he did not appreciate.

The revolution in Peking opera that he began—or that his wife conducted beginning in 1962–63—was an attempt to regain control of the propaganda machine and to stop the

[2] Originating from the audience.

criticism, which could have sapped his power. Also, at this time, he began to fear that some of his colleagues were preparing reports aimed at destroying his reputation, such as that delivered by Khrushchev in 1956 to denounce Stalin. These anxieties motivated him as he intensified the drive to regain power in 1964 or early 1965, which culminated in the Cultural Revolution.

QUESTION: To what extent has the Peking regime been able to protect China's scientific structure and program in the face of the Cultural Revolution, and what is the state of education in China? It has been reliably reported that virtually all education is confined to the study of Mao's sayings. If that is the case, how can a country develop with such limited training?

OANCIA: The impression I had before I left was that parts of the scientific community were fairly well insulated from the excesses of the Cultural Revolution, particularly those segments dealing with defense science, the atomic energy program, and probably the missile program. Many other sectors in the scientific world were not protected; members of the medical profession suffered greatly. The medical institutes in Peking were pretty badly battered during the rather violent phases in 1967 and early 1968. Peking Union Medical College, the old institute that was founded with American financial help, was badly hit.

The technical university in Peking, Tsinghua University, had some pretty terrible battles about the time I left. Rival groups of Red Guards were fighting among themselves, smashing windows, ripping out radiators in the classrooms. They even burned down some of the buildings.

Education, as we know it in this part of the world, really was not being conducted at all. However, by about the beginning of 1968, there was a determined effort to get students back into school. As for the curriculum, the study of the thought of Mao Tse-tung took up most of the time. There was some emphasis on arithmetic, elementary Chinese language training, and some of the basic sciences, but no real program had been developed for the universities or even for the secondary schools.

MAC FARQUHAR: One of Mao's major aims is to move toward a more egalitarian society. The educational system in its pre–Cultural Revolution form, which in China certainly resembled that in the West, although obviously there were many differences, tended to favor the children of middle-class families—the children, in the case of China, of Communist Party officials, bureaucrats, and so on. The children of workers and peasants did not start with enough basic knowledge to get into universities. One of the striking experiments that the Chinese seem to be making is the abolition of entrance criteria in order to try and make university education more egalitarian.

PFEFFER: I would like to put the Chinese educational system, or the lack of it at this moment, in comparative perspective. In the first place, the notion of work-study, one of the dominant themes of Mao's approach to education, has been increasingly espoused by so-called avant-garde educators around the world. Secondly, the question of whether one's education is relevant is surely at the heart of the student movement in the United States, in France, and in almost every major country in the world. Thirdly, the authority of the professor or the teacher who gives the "word"—an especially serious problem in China, where "the word" has always been so sacred—is also of universal scope. This issue of authority raises the whole question of the nature of institutions and how participatory they should be.

The very important factor of Mao's ideology in China, which one can understand even if one is not terribly enthusiastic about it, should not be overlooked. But I think the central question raised by the Cultural Revolution, and by the educational reforms that have been carried out and will be carried out, is a question of participatory institutions. This central question was raised by Eugene McCarthy in his own way and will increasingly be raised in the United States.

QUESTION: Can a revolution be created or manipulated or manufactured? Isn't this a contradiction in terms? Isn't a revolution supposed to be spontaneous? Furthermore, in attempting to institutionalize revolution, Mao seems to be seeking to change human nature. Is this possible? Can one demand constant sacrifices from the people without promising them a piece of the pie? Why does Mao think he can pressure and control his movement after his own death?

PFEFFER: As the Cultural Revolution makes clear, a man cannot create and manipulate a revolution. He can influence it; he can play on various kinds of dissatisfaction in the attempt to channel the revolution; but, as the revolution subverts existing institutions, the leader runs the risk of losing all control, of having to allow organizations and interest groups at the bottom to determine the course of the revolution.

But Mao did not have to create a "new" revolution. This is not a case where Mao had to wage a revolution in the classic sense. The Chinese have already been through their classic revolution. They effectively eliminated the pre-Communist ruling class before 1950. In the Cultural Revolution, Mao has been trying to release pent-up social forces in the hope that under his leadership they would propel the Chinese revolution in the "proper" direction again.

I agree that the problem of institutionalizing revolution is essentially a problem of human nature. It is a problem with which many of the great political theorists of the past have been concerned. But it is not a problem for which there are neat or universal solutions.

Obviously, the problem of creating a successor generation and passing control of the revolution to them is part of the larger issue of institutionalizing the revolution. Succession in China frequently has been discussed in terms of the difficulty of passing on Mao's charisma. Lin Piao, if he does succeed to the leadership of the Party, will not have the same charismatic leadership quality as Mao. This is one reason why Mao is trying to institutionalize his revolutionary vision and style.

QUESTION: I understand the compatibility between mass egalitarianism and participation and a very severe program of indoctrination, but how can a strenuous indoctrination program lead to spontaneity on the part of the people? Mr. Mac-Farquhar, to what extent has the Cultural Revolution had spontaneity?

MAC FARQUHAR: The question of maintaining spontaneity in the Cultural Revolution is another aspect of what I would call the complexity of Mao and the complexity of the problems he faces. If spontaneity is the goal, it is an obvious contradiction to keep telling people that the words of one man and one leader are the ultimate truth. China, however, has an enormous number of people whom it is very difficult to move. As in the army, the larger the body of men you want to move, the louder the officer shouts. In the case of China, he is shouting very loudly indeed. And he is shouting in very simple terms. We talk about the "little red book," the "selected works," the indoctrination of Maoism. A great deal of it boils down to very simple precepts, which can be grasped extremely easily: for instance, the need for selfless labor on behalf of your fellow men, the belief that man can change nature. The latter idea is extremely important in a country like China where the people have always seen nature as the dominant force.

During the Great Leap Forward and on other occasions, obviously this indoctrination has been carried to an extreme. But if Mao left behind only one idea in the minds of his fellow Chinese—namely, that by effort, by will, they can eventually change their world—this is an idea, it would seem to me, that has yet to be grasped by the people of many other countries of Asia at a similar stage of development. On the other hand, what Mao wants is 700 million men all like himself, embracing such ideas but at the same time acting with initiative and spontaneity. Presumably, Mao hopes that eventually his countrymen will be imbued so thoroughly with his ideas that, when using their initiative on specific occasions, they will act precisely as he himself would have done.

QUESTION: China's youth thought that they would play a significant role in post–Cultural Revolution China, but the current moves toward retrenchment, moderation, and consolidation have curtailed their exuberant participation in Chinese affairs. When the students are directed, as they have been, to go back to school and obey the teachers they have attacked just a few months before, will there not be cynicism? What will this mean for the future?

OANCIA: I think there is going to be a considerable amount of cynicism among youths first instructed to rebel and attack authorities, including teachers, and then ordered to desist and return to the classroom. There are really two problems: How are the students going to respond when they go back to school, and how are the teachers going to behave when *they* go back to school?

From firsthand experience, I know something about the teachers' response. They are terrified. They will do almost anything to avoid going back to the classroom. I think some of them have even asked to be sent out to the countryside to work on communes or to work in factories rather than return to school to face possible uprisings, resistance, and violent treatment from their students.

Since the tamping down of the Cultural Revolution, there has been a mass exodus of students from the cities to the frontier areas and to the areas that the Chinese authorities feel should be populated. Possibly some of the people who would be most active in leading students' criticism of teachers are those who have ended up in the deserts of Sinkiang or in the marshes of Heilungkiang.

MAC FARQUHAR: Vis à vis the youth, I think the first thing

Mao has attempted to do is to make the present generation of Red Guards realize that they can only be, to use Daniel Cohn-Bendit's [3] term, "the detonators." They cannot be the continuers. The working class must be the continuers. As for the future, I think Mao may feel that old men may remember the past but young men forget and that within one or two generations' time, the frustrations and the needs will not have disappeared, and young people will be ready to rise again as Red Guards, if there is someone to inspire them.

WALKER: We attribute so much to the "great helmsman," to the great leader Chairman Mao. What we may actually have been seeing in the last ten years is the manipulation of a Mao cult by a fair number of people. We simply do not know what is going on and what is taking place in his name in China, nor do the Chinese for that matter. His daily life is a complete secret. How much influence Ch'en Po-ta, his former political secretary and speech-writer, or Chiang Ch'ing, his wife, or other people have, or to what extent political power has been manipulated in the name of a man who obviously cannot have done all the things that are attributed to him is just uncertain. Mao is an old man; he has been sick; he does not have that much energy. When we try to interpret the events of this very diverse country in which many political forces are at work as Mao doing this or Mao doing that, we make a great mistake. I just do not think we know.

QUESTION: Is there similarity between the effects of Stalinism and the resulting moderation in Russia and events now transpiring in China? What do you see as the principal significance of China's nuclear ambitions for China's internal politics and foreign policies? Do Mao and the people behind him have the power to wage successful war against the Soviet Union?

[3] Daniel Cohn-Bendit was a student leader during the French student-worker uprisings of the spring of 1968.

KREISBERG: China's conflicting policy and ideological interests are reflected internally in the opposing views of large numbers of people. This is one of the things that the Cultural Revolution has been about. One of the groups that lost power during the Cultural Revolution may have been in favor of a more moderate foreign policy or perhaps one that could accurately be described as a more nationalist policy. Perhaps such a policy would really be more moderate, perhaps it would not. For example, I can envisage a highly nationalistic China that, in terms of its propensity to attack neighbors, to enlarge its territory, to assert its national power, might be much more of a threat in terms of the risk of war.

Obviously, one of the central strands of our policy toward China is the hope that, over time, the Chinese will become less interested or less involved in the pursuit of a revolutionary foreign policy, a policy of actively encouraging revolutions in other countries.

As a country, the United States is primarily concerned with carrying out policies and conducting relations with other countries on a bilateral, state-to-state basis. There would obviously still be many problems in dealing with Peking on such terms, but, if the Chinese once begin thinking of the world primarily in this way, rather than as a global revolutionary battlefield, the prospects for clarifying and resolving such bilateral problems and for reducing tensions in Asia may improve.

The primary effect of China's nuclear policy on its domestic affairs is one of cost. The development of an arsenal of nuclear weapons is extremely expensive. The totality of China's resource base is very large, but China's ability to mobilize its resources is limited. The problem of how to allocate these resources may have been one of the factors, in the middle 1960's, behind the decision to carry out the Cultural Revolution. For many years, there has been a debate within Peking over the portions of the national pie that should be allocated to defense, to domestic economic construction, and to foreign aid. Thus far, the Chinese have acted on the belief that their national defense and the power image they wish to project require that they continue to develop nuclear weapons. This obviously pares away funds they could use for needed technology and technicians for other purposes. We have, of course, heard much the same argument with regard to the United States, but our political system is better arranged than Peking's for peacefully resolving such controversies.

QUESTION: I am Louis Fischer of Princeton University. I lived through a "cultural revolution" in the Soviet Union—it was not called that, but that is what it was.

I was interested in what Mr. Kreisberg of the State Department said, and I was surprised that he was so realistic. Then he disappointed me when he claimed that the normalization of China—its becoming nationalist and giving up world revolution—would make it easier to deal with. I think it is quite the contrary. The Soviet Union was easier to deal with when it was talking about world revolution. It became much more difficult to deal with when it became nationalistic and then imperialistic. So I take no comfort from the prospect of China's becoming more nationalistic.

One thing that has not been mentioned is China's disinterest in world affairs, in international relations. In contrast, the Soviet Union was eager to establish relations with foreign countries, to be recognized. The Russians bribed Mussolini to recognize them. They fought during the 1920's and 1930's to take part in international affairs. The Russians from time immemorial had had an inferiority complex toward the outside world, especially toward the West. But China is the "middle kingdom"; it is a world in itself; it does not want to have foreign relations. And this, I think, is the problem. This is the source of blunders in the State Department.

Why doesn't the U.S. Government say we want the People's Republic in the United Nations? I doubt whether Peking would accept such a proposal, but it would take the burden from us, because the mainland Chinese would not agree to join the United Nations so long as Taiwan represented China in the organization.

I think, therefore, that while Mr. Kreisberg was quite realistic, the State Department and the U.S. Government, irrespective of the party in control, have not been realistic in our China policy.

KREISBERG: Mr. Fischer seems to have praised me for not sounding like the Department of State. I am not going to comment specifically on his question, because I think that it will be taken up in considerably more detail in a later panel.

But I would like to say one thing about his observation about China as a national state versus China as a revolutionary state. I do not disagree with him. I think that in many ways China may pose a great many new and even more difficult problems for a period of time, once it turns its attention to dealing with other states as states, and for some of the reasons that he described.

When China begins to look at its relations with other countries in terms of the whole complex of its national interests, including economic development, its need for trade, and the desirability of living in a peaceful environment, however, we will be able to have greater confidence in its decisions, for China will then be functioning more in terms of the basic considerations that govern our own thought processes.

China has not been very interested in foreign affairs and has had a highly Sino-centric view of the world for 2,000 years. I think this is one of the reasons why China's attitude toward dealing with other countries has provided so many difficulties for those countries. I continue to be optimistic, however, that over a period of time this may change.

MAC FARQUHAR: I would like to disagree briefly with both Mr. Kreisberg's and Mr. Fischer's statements that China is not interested in world affairs. China has shown itself, especially in the last few years, not interested in foreign *relations* perhaps or in contact between Peking and other capitals in the conventional sense, but Mao Tse-tung and his leadership group in Peking are profoundly interested in *world affairs*. The major thrust of the Cultural Revolution is to purify China so that it may be the bastion of world revolution. While Mao *is* interested in world revolution, this does not mean that he is going to send troops across the frontiers to promote it. But he is profoundly interested in world affairs. To think that he is not is a fundamental mistake.

QUESTION: Professor Pfeffer, do you think that the United States can develop a reasonable and wise policy toward China? Can the two countries have normal and peaceful relations without a basic change in the political, economic, and social conditions within the United States?

PFEFFER: My reaction to that question is mixed. I basically believe that the answer is no. But I would hate to rule out the kinds of reasonable things that we could do if we had the will. I suppose that I have not yet wholly accepted any so-called ideological explanations of what the United States is and does. I still have some hope that we can change our policies. There are, after all, a number of simple things that we can do. We can, for example, withdraw all our bases from Asia. I do not believe that the capitalist system makes it inevitable that we must be imperialists. And even if it were true that imperialists we must be, I fail to understand why we cannot be smarter about it. Why, with the developments in transportation, communications, military technology, and weaponry, can we not withdraw? I suppose that I am too far away from the internal workings of government to comprehend the bureaucratic mentality.

But, to answer your question in a different way, I do not think that we have any choice. The United States is going to change whether we like it or not. And I, at least, expect to like it. I am willing to take a chance on what change may bring. The United States will change because there are enough dis-

parate elements in this country who are fed up with our domestic and foreign policies. There are so many things that
we can do now. We could have made a start at this convocation.

QUESTION: Is Chou En-lai likely to be an influence in the
years ahead? Will he have much influence over Lin Piao, for
example, after Mao dies?

MAC FARQUHAR: While Mao has produced the great direc-
tives and has been helped in this by his wife and secretary,
what Chou En-lai has done is to work about 26 hours a day
attempting both to keep alongside Mao in the Cultural Revolution and to keep the country together. In fact, in a leadership group of considerable eminence, two men, it seems to
me, have emerged as giants, and one of them is Chou En-lai.
Over the past three years, he has displayed incredible energy
for a man of seventy, going on seventy-one. He is still a power.

II.
China
and
World
Security

LINCOLN P. BLOOMFIELD

In recent years the official U.S. picture of China's world role has not been accepted by many other countries; indeed, China's proper place in the world security equation is widely disputed in this country. Opinions vary from those who see Peking as an implacably belligerent, revolutionary, racist, xenophobic, expansionist power that is only waiting for an ICBM capability to smash American cities all the way to those who feel China is just another developing country whose leadership is romantic, prudent, and justifiably obsessed with China's security because of U.S. hostility. Presumably truth lies somewhere between the extremes.

It must include China's burgeoning nuclear weapons capacity and the need to refashion our notions of strategic bargaining and mutual deterrence to encompass a triangular U.S.-China-U.S.S.R. relationship. Another fact is China's pressure on some of its neighbors, as well as Peking's sense of grievance at the unequal treaties that have produced borders about which it quarrels. Yet another fact is its exclusion from all the world forums where international peace and security are regularly discussed.

In order to clarify some basic American assumptions and define a rational and informed American strategic posture toward China, such key issues as the realities of Chinese military capabilities, the strategic view from Peking, the effect on China's posture of polycentric Communist rivalries, China's external policies in Asia and the Pacific, and the implications and choices for U.S. policy will be explored in the following pages.

SAMUEL B. GRIFFITH 2ND

Any discussion of the realities of China's military capacity must begin with the fact that, for more than two years, the three services, particularly the army, and, to a lesser degree, the navy and air force, have been deeply involved in the Great Proletarian Cultural Revolution. The People's Liberation Army (PLA) has been injected into every aspect of Chinese life and society, and it is loyal to Party Chairman Mao Tse-tung and his Minister of Defense and heir designate, Lin Piao.

The PLA actually controls all provincial revolutionary committees. The armed forces are now overseeing (if not actually operating) factories, mines, railroads, shipping, civil airlines, the postal and telegraphic services, schools and universities, the motion picture industry, radio, television, the newspapers, and even the celebrated Peking opera. The army is also playing important propaganda, production, and military training roles in thousands of rural villages.

This extracurricular activity has absorbed and will continue to absorb a large percentage of the army's manpower, time, and energies. Thus, there has been a progressive, severe diminution in the combat capabilities of China's ground forces.

The development of complex and expensive strategic systems, such as airborne and amphibious ones, are not within the capabilities of the People's Republic and will not be for at least two decades. Thus, the ability of the People's Republic to project its conventional military power beyond immediate peripheral areas is limited. Constraints of terrain and logistics would further impair these capabilities.

For the foreseeable future, the strategy of the People's Republic will be one of "walking on two legs": encouragement and support of "people's wars" to the extent possible and further development of strategic offensive nuclear forces. Of the limited funds available for conventional forces, the bulk will go to air defense: early warning interceptor aircraft, antiaircraft rockets and guns, and command and control systems —all of which are extremely expensive to design, develop, and produce and absorb a large number of scientists, engineers, and technicians who might be more productively employed in other sectors of the economy.

It is prudent to assume that Chinese progress in the development of its nuclear deterrent continues. If any program was insulated from the excesses of the Cultural Revolution, it was the nuclear program. While no one is certain in which direction this program is going to move, an intercontinental bomber system—that is, a long-range, manned bomber system which is expensive and already obsolescent in both the United States and the Soviet Union—is out. This nevertheless leaves several options, such as a seaborne submarine delivery system equipped with cruise missiles, ballistic missiles of about 1,000-nautical-mile range, or an ICBM similar to our *Minuteman.* Clandestine delivery should not be discounted, but, if used, it would probably be in conjunction with one or both of the other systems mentioned.

Washington seems wedded to the theory that China will go

to the ICBM system, and experts reasonably estimate that China could have perhaps fifty such missiles by 1975 or 1976. China could also by that time have a somewhat larger stockpile of 1,000-mile missiles, which Peking might be foolish enough to believe it could use in blackmailing its Asian neighbors.

By the mid-1970's, China might be amenable to discussing nuclear arms control. This would depend on several variables, such as the orientation of the Peking leadership at the time, the state of the triangular relationship between the United States, the Soviet Union, and the People's Republic, the orientation of the Soviet and American leaders, and, finally, the Chinese estimate of the credibility of its nuclear deterrent in U.S. and Soviet eyes. At present, no one in Moscow, Washington, or Peking can forecast the shape of these variables. After Mao goes, as he soon must, the future possibilities of an arms control arrangement should gradually be clarified. The U.S. Government is working on many possibilities for eventual arms control that would involve Communist China, but, until Mao goes, arms control arrangements with the People's Republic appear to be foreclosed.

ALLEN S. WHITING

No longer can one talk about "China" or the "Chinese," for the Cultural Revolution has shown that at least three different clusters of personalities and decision-making groups have interacted in the formulation and implementation of policy.

One group might be identified as Mao Tse-tung and the Cultural Revolution ideologues. The second group would comprise Liu Shao-ch'i and the civilian components of the bureaucracy. Premier Chou En-lai and almost certainly Ch'en I, the former Foreign Minister, probably figure in this group. The third group could be called the professional military leadership and would include such men as the two former Ministers of Defense—P'eng Teh-huai, who was purged in 1959 for confronting Mao Tse-tung on the Great Leap Forward policies, and Lo Jui-ch'ing, who was purged in 1965–66, also for confronting Mao over policy.

To say that three separate groups exist, however, is not to preclude points of agreement within the leadership nor to deny the possibility of projecting from the present to the future. It is safe to assume that there is a high level of agreement among these clusters of decision-makers on the Sino-centric basis of achieving equality with other powers, to the extent that that is possible, and superiority, where that is possible.

If they focus on the nuclear component in particular, they know that in 1953, as revealed by the memoirs of President Eisenhower, the United States delivered a veiled nuclear threat to the Chinese Communists that unless the Korean War was ended forthwith, the United States would consider the use of nuclear weapons in the northern half of the Korean peninsula. This may not have been what compelled them to agree to American terms at that time (Stalin died at about that time), but this was at least communicated to Peking. They know that in 1958 America continued its intervention in the Chinese civil war by providing the Chinese Nationalist troops on Quemoy with 8-inch howitzers capable of handling nuclear shells. In so doing, the United States reminded the Chinese that nuclear weapons are today's counterpart of the nineteenth-century gunboat.

The Chinese leadership groups have differed on the means of acquiring their own nuclear capability—the degree to which China has to go it alone or place itself under the Soviet nuclear umbrella. They have differed, in other words, on operational and foreign-policy aspects. At least two chiefs of staff seem to have advocated greater reliance on the Soviet deterrent and on Soviet nuclear aid than Mao was willing to tolerate.

One recurring theme in the strategic debate in Peking is the threat of foreign exploitation of Chinese vulnerabilities. Chinese history of the nineteenth century and experiences with foreign powers in the twentieth century have engendered in the Chinese a deep conviction that, if China is weak or down, some country will take advantage of this. They would differ, however, on how to react to such a situation. Mao might argue for a pre-emptive posture of militant vigilance. At a time of weakness, one shows one's fiercest face to the enemy; in fact, certain actions on China's borders, which would otherwise be considered provocative and aggressive, might be advisable. But, in his view, this action would be strictly aimed at pre-empting an enemy thrust. Others in the leadership might prefer a tactical divide-the-enemy approach, which emphasizes diplomacy and building China's case with as many allies as possible in order to make the enemy less willing to move against it.

Another area in which there have been differences that might be projected into the future is the question of the degree to which revolutions in third-world countries are to be supported, with the attendant risk to China, as opposed to the enhancement of China's power through more conventional diplomatic means. Mere capability alone does not determine the degree of force the Chinese put into people's wars; a more complicated mix of considerations is involved. The fact that the Chinese have offered little armed force to support people's wars on their borders suggests that the mouthings of the ideologues do not carry over into the areas of military policy.

The Chinese leadership, in other words, must be seen as a pluralistic elite, which will be in flux and which will be reacting to what the United States does, as well as to what it sees as its own opportunities. Whether the U.S. posture is one of confrontation or compromise is likely to make a significant difference in the choice of means and, particularly, in the use of force by the Chinese leadership.

While any significant Chinese use of force to support local insurrections appears unlikely, its use in border disputes is a recurring problem, which both Indians and Russians must deal with if they remain in dispute with the Chinese over border areas. In addition, there is the use of force in civil wars—in this case between the Chinese Communists and the Chinese Nationalists. The United States intervened in the Chinese civil war in 1950. Washington used its political and military power to stop that fighting, literally within eyesight of the mainland of China, on the offshore islands of Quemoy and Matsu. There is no guarantee that force will not be tested in this particular area over the next decade.

In sum, the Chinese have used force consonant with what they perceive as vital interests—in Korea massively and in Vietnam selectively.[1] This is not irrational behavior. And it is not behavior that suggests an irrevocable commitment to use the force at their initiative. But it is behavior that suggests that the Chinese must be reckoned with and dealt with, as indeed any world power should be.

[1] Beginning in the fall of 1965 and ending in the summer of 1969, China dispatched up to 50,000 regular PLA troops to North Vietnam. These troops were primarily engineers and construction workers for building and repairing roads, railroads, airfields, and supply bases, but they did include anti-aircraft divisions, which fired on U.S. aircraft attacking North Vietnam.

FRANZ MICHAEL

The threat posed by Communist China to the peace of the world is caused by the instability of Maoism and the uncertainty of the future of China's Communist regime. This uncertainty makes it impossible to speak of China as a given entity whose actions are reasonably predictable and to which a policy could be related. Ever since the beginning of the Cultural Revolution, Communist China has been in the throes of a major political upheaval, which affects the entire foundation of its social, economic, and intellectual order. The outcome is clearly not yet determined.

A revolution of the kind started by Mao against China's own Communist system is unheard of in the history of Communism. Normally, the Communist revolution occurs in the first years after takeover and is directed against all social groups that might stand in the way of the establishment of a new Communist order. In China, too, the years of the great drives, between 1949 and 1953, saw the elimination of vast numbers of people in preparation for the establishment of a political structure that followed the model of the Soviet Union and the Eastern European Communist countries. Communism was to come in a phased development with five-year planning, under a social order directed by a Chinese Marxist-Leninist Party that formed part of what was at that time regarded as a combined Communist bloc and movement. Mao and the Sino-Soviet conflict changed all that.

Beginning with the Great Leap Forward in 1958 and again with the Cultural Revolution, Mao has attempted to put his own stamp on a new concept of revolution, first for China and then for the world. His is "instant Communism," to be achieved not by stages of development but by sheer will-power and organization under a revolutionary strategy derived from the precepts of the strategy of wars of liberation.

National liberation movements and wars of national liberation were the form under which Communism was to advance in the nonindustrial countries of the Afro-Asian world. It was a strategy for the conquest of power. What Mao has done is to return to it after years of Communist rule in China. To re-establish his power when he felt challenged both from within his own Party and from Moscow, he used the instrument of military power to impose his own authority over that of the Chinese Communist Party. Through the build-up of the thought of Mao Tse-tung and the deification of himself, Mao has attempted to establish a cult of personality wherein he ascribes to himself the possession of historical truth, which in Marxist-Leninist doctrine has always resided in the Party. Mao has thus combined into one the two sides of the totalitarian coin, Marxism-Leninism and the leader cult. With the help of the military, he has attempted to indoctrinate a fanatical following—first the Red Guards, then the revolutionary rebels,[1] now the Mao-thought propaganda teams,[2] and, most

---

[1] In distinction to the Red Guards, who were originally college and high school students, the revolutionary rebels were a combined group, including young and ambitious Maoists in the offices of the government, the communes, and the factories. They were organized by the military, in combination with the Red Guards, for the "seizure of power" in 1967.

[2] Teams composed primarily of workers and PLA men were dispatched to schools and universities to instruct the students in the thought of Mao.

of all, the military itself—for the propagation of his concepts and the establishment of his authority. If he succeeds, his will be the ultimate in totalitarianism.

It is clearly not only a matter of Chinese domestic interest if Maoism claims to represent the new formula of revolution for the peoples of the world. Mao's appeal, sloganized in more than 750 million copies of the little red book, is meant to incite the peoples of the world to a revolutionary rising against their governments and social order. But this dream of Peking as the new center of world revolution and of Mao as prophet appears to have little reality outside the thinking of the present Chinese leadership and of some youthful cult seekers among the world's quasi-intellectuals.

The success of Maoism in China itself is by no means assured. As of now, the new Maoism appears in control in Communist China. The Party and government structure has disintegrated under the Maoist attacks and has been largely replaced by the military and the revolutionary committees. A new Maoist Party is in the making. Loyalty to Mao is the only criterion for membership; whoever is for Mao is proletarian; whoever is against him is bourgeois. A new leap is propagated throughout the nation. Mao is again attempting to abolish all private property and private economic activities; all personal advantages and incentives are rejected. Organization and political purpose replace progress and economic development. To maintain a working order under this political line, social group after social group in China has been forced into the wilderness, but the battle continues as proclaimed by the Maoists themselves. "Struggle-criticism-transformation" is carried on constantly and will be carried on for many years to come.

Meanwhile, the majority of the Red Guards, once the little generals of the revolution, have been sent to the rural areas to live with the peasants for the rest of their lives. School graduates, professors, and intellectuals have been similarly banished to the countryside in a military-backed Maoist move. In the latest mass movement, millions of people from the cities—the claim is 30 per cent of the urban population—have been transplanted to rural communities. The alienation and disruption created by this social manipulation has clearly assumed massive proportions, and one must wonder about the accumulation of explosive resentment in what can only be regarded as a latent revolutionary situation.

While it is conceivable that Maoism will continue to prevail as it has heretofore, no leader cult has so far survived the death of its leader. The question is: What will happen after Mao's death, or even earlier, should his control weaken? Will the military, the main tool of power today, remain unified and be able to hold things together? What political purpose, what ideology would cement a nation that has undergone such extraordinary trials? Could Maoist utopianism prevail under Lin Piao or another military leader? Can a Marxist-Leninist Party make a comeback? Will the trend toward decentralization and regionalism, already apparent today, lead to disintegration, conflict, or even civil war? It appears to this observer that years of turmoil are just as likely to lie ahead as is any success in maintaining unity under Maoism, Communism, or nationalism, in unalloyed or hybrid form.

The future of China will be decided inside China and will be determined by the opposing social, political, and military forces. But outside action could contribute to and affect the outcome. It is therefore of great importance that this situation be understood before any decision on policy with regard to mainland China is made. Unless a clear decision to influence the power struggle is made—and this would be at best a risky business—the only possible attitude must be hands off. Any political involvement today appears unpredictable in outcome and an unnecessary limitation on future freedom of action. It is not now a question of establishing formal relations with China. With which force in China are relations to be established? And what effect would such relations have on the outcome of the internal conflict in Communist China? A recognition of the Chinese Maoist government today will, in effect, not be a recognition of "China," let alone its 750 million people whom we would like to reach, but will be a recognition of Mao's new type of government and a move related to the internal power struggle. It may not even be acceptable to the Maoist regime.

Other reasons make it impractical to go beyond the present contacts and extend a friendly hand to Mao Tse-tung. It is utterly unrealistic to expect that the United States can reconcile such action with its existing responsibilities in the Far East. America has nothing to gain and much to lose in current support from Far Eastern nations if it abandons its commitments.

Any intervention in opposition to Mao, on the other hand, would be equally foolhardy and would only unify contending forces. The massive Chinese demonstrations following the frontier incident at the Ussuri River have been interpreted as an attempt by Peking to rally support to the Maoist side for the Ninth Party Congress by pointing to a possible military danger from the Soviet Union.

The build-up of thermonuclear power in China is continuing and is of concern, and it poses the threat of irrational action, but Communist China will hardly be strong enough in the foreseeable future to compete in world affairs on a true power basis. The setback of the Cultural Revolution and the sheer waste of human and economic resources have worsened China's already difficult position and have further handicapped the race between economic and population growth. What is to be feared is not so much a Chinese attack as the effect of a Chinese crisis on world affairs and on the relations between the free world and the Soviet orbit.

The new Soviet doctrine of limited sovereignty within the Socialist commonwealth and of the right of intervention in the alleged defense of socialism against threat from within or without has raised the specter of Soviet intervention should the Chinese crisis deepen. China is no Czechoslovakia, but its most important areas of thermonuclear development and military industry are very vulnerable to Soviet action. The Chinese accusation against the new "socialist imperialism" of the Soviet Union is based on fear. World security may be threatened as much in China as in the Near East. For the United States, it may be wise not only to keep hands off but to secure in discussions of global issues with the Soviet Union an assurance of mutual nonintervention.

The issue is not one of enticing a leader-cult to change—which would be futile—but of keeping options open to cope with a decision in China, which, it is hoped, will halt the present trend. This trend is dangerous for the world and a terrible fate for the Chinese people who deserve better.

CHESTER L. COOPER

The areas of chief concern, the areas of existing or potential tension, the points that may be conceivable targets of offensive or even defensive thrusts by China's conventional military forces include, first, Taiwan and the offshore islands. To China, these clearly represent unfinished business. So long as they are occupied and governed by the Chinese Nationalists, the civil war goes on. Furthermore, Peking perceives these hostile enclaves as incipient threats to the mainland. Second, the China-India border is still an unresolved problem, with troops of both sides concentrated in that area. Third, the thirty-eighth parallel in Korea remains an uneasy truce line. There is always the threat that the South Koreans or North Koreans, by design or by miscalculation, will resume the hostilities that were halted but not definitely resolved fifteen years ago. Large-scale Korean fighting would almost certainly result in American and Chinese forces in combat once again. Finally, it is unlikely—but not inconceivable—that China might find the situation in a post-settlement North Vietnam intolerable to it, but, more likely, Peking's desire to increase the pressure on Thailand may make Laos, Burma, and Cambodia vulnerable to Chinese military moves. One need only read the morning newspaper to be reminded of the apparent hostility of the situation on the long Chinese-Soviet border.

China's capabilities to move major military forces against these areas are not uniform. The present amphibious capability of the Chinese Communist navy would not support the assault and follow-on echelons of a force large enough to make a decisive attack on Taiwan. If merchant and fishing craft were added to the amphibious fleet, there would still be very difficult problems of air and fire support. The not inconsiderable Chinese Nationalist navy would have to be reckoned with, but the intercession of the U.S. Seventh Fleet would make the venture hopeless. Peking must also recognize that the extensive shipbuilding, equipping, and training programs required to support a major amphibious assault would be bound to attract U.S. attention at a fairly early point.

Operations against the offshore islands, particularly Quemoy, would also be hard to conceal during the preparatory stages of an assault. A major attempt could succeed, but these islands are now well enough defended to cause the Communists massive casualties if they attack. Uncertainties over the American reaction would induce some caution, particularly in light of the 1958 experience. Intensive bombardment of the offshore islands could be resumed at any time, but the returns would appear to be low.

Airborne operations of any size, specifically against India, are beyond the reach of the Chinese at this time. Their inventory of transport aircraft cannot lift a large enough force to maintain itself at any significant point within India.

The Korean intervention showed very clearly the Chinese capability to mobilize large forces in that area. Should the

North Koreans together with the Chinese choose to move again, the United States would be faced with difficult decisions. The question of using tactical nuclear weapons could arise very early in the defense of Seoul. In addition, the continued use of American bases in Japan can by no means now be taken for granted.

Although problems of logistics in other areas of interest to the United States in Asia would tend to reduce the size of the force the Chinese might choose to employ in any specific case, they could still inject ground forces of significant size. China would encounter especially significant limitations if it attempted an attack of major proportions against India below the mountain areas. At points closer to its borders, however, China could probably seize sizable areas rather quickly, despite India's claims that it has increased its border defenses.

Before Peking attacked one of the smaller Asian nations on its border, Chinese planners would have to calculate the likelihood and the effect of an American response not only in terms of face-to-face contact in the battle area but also in terms of the nature of the total battleground exposed by the Chinese action. In the face of overt Chinese aggression against an American ally, China's lines of communication would almost certainly come under U.S. air attack. More significantly, the United States would probably carry the attack to China's nuclear, military, and industrial installations.

If, as current conditions seem to suggest, China's real problem lies along its borders with the Soviet Union, the Chinese will not behave aggressively in other areas. However, with the Chinese heavily engaged with Russian forces, the Chinese Nationalists might be tempted to exploit the situation and launch an attack against China's southeast coast. Under the circumstances, China probably would be very cautious about getting involved in a two-front war, but Chinese Communist attacks on U.S. forces in the area could nevertheless result.

On balance, Chinese preoccupation with the Cultural Revolution and conditions stemming from it, together with current tension with the Soviet Union, will reduce the prospects of Chinese conventional ground forces acting against other nations along China's border.

In terms of costs and benefits, the Chinese should regard support of "people's wars" or "wars of national liberation" as their best investment. Such activities require the United States to commit substantial resources to a variety of undertakings, while the Chinese, at comparatively low cost and risk, maintain unstable situations and promote their own causes.

The threat of Chinese long-range military action, amphibious or airborne, is for the time being minimal. The Chinese are capable of intervention along and over their borders and could pose a serious problem for the United States, but there is a conservative cast to Chinese policy that suggests that provocation of a serious nature would be required first.

If the Nixon Administration, unlike the previous one, chooses to take a hard new look at relations with China, it must confront some difficult questions. For example, what of the policy of "containment"? What, in practical, operational terms, does "containment without isolation" mean? Does the United States regard a major clash between Peking and Moscow as a spectator sport? What about Taiwan, now and after Chiang? What new possibilities exist for establishing a *modus vivendi* with China after Mao? Should some new options be proposed now so that a new Chinese leadership can consider them before they assume power? Now that the role of arch-villain seems to be shifting to Moscow, should Washington present a new face to China? And, if it does, what happens to U.S. relations with Moscow and to the high hopes for a meaningful détente with the Soviet Union?

The task before the United States involves, first, the maintenance of a posture and policies that will discourage Chinese use of sizable conventional forces in areas of concern to the United States. Second, and most important, Washington must assist those nations whose security is imperiled by covert Chinese action. American assistance must be largely non-military and aimed at the achievement of social order and progress of such quality as to negate the Chinese alternative.

DISCUSSION

BLOOMFIELD: Before we go any further with predictions, analyses, estimates, and forecasts, I would ask whether or not we recognize that not only Chinese decision-making but American as well involves some psychology. How, when we talk about the future and lay out the lines of American policy, do we keep in mind any stereotypes we may have about China as a traditional friend—or enemy? About the past U.S. role in Asia? About racial relations? How do we avoid being prisoners of our own past images and policies, when we may need entirely new ones?

GRIFFITH: Let us imagine for a moment that we are sitting in Peking. We will take a look around and see whether we like what we see or not.

Let us look first to the north, across Manchuria to the Ussuri River, where the Soviet Far Eastern Army is deployed along a front of 1,000 miles around the tip of Manchuria. I do not know what the order of battle is, but they have plenty of motorized infantry and armor and no doubt a very strong tactical air force. In South Korea, two American divisions are supported by tactical aircraft, and nuclear weapons are available. To the east, American bases stand ready in Japan and on Okinawa. Then, dropping down a little further, we see Taiwan, supported by the U.S. Seventh Fleet ranging the Pacific, and nuclear submarines armed with *Poseidon* missiles in sufficient quantity no doubt to destroy all the major cities of China. Drop down a little further and look at anti-Chinese movements in the Philippines. The Philippine Government is being very stringent; the Chinese say that they are lackeys of American imperialism. To the South, in Vietnam, are almost 600,-000 Americans, including air force and naval combat units. Then, south of the Himalayas is hostile India, and, along the other 3,000 miles to the west, the Soviet Army is again deployed.

If we were sitting on the Standing Committee of the Politburo or on the Military Affairs Commission in Peking, would we be apprehensive or would we not?

BLOOMFIELD: In addition to these armed preparations around China's periphery, President Nixon has proposed the installation within the United States of a modified version of the *Sentinel* antiballistic missile (ABM). What are the implications of this proposal in terms of the U.S.-Chinese strategic relationship? Why are we building an antiballistic missile system that is supposed to be anti-Chinese?

COOPER: An antiballistic missile as a thin defense against China is nonsense from several points of view. The idea was originally conceived of during the previous Administration as a rationalization for not wanting to spend enough for an ABM system that could provide effective defense against the Soviet Union. Although there is much controversy and confusion over the ABM issue, one aspect seems clear: we apparently are unable to afford the cost of building a system that would offer total defense against Soviet missiles. I do not think we need a thin ABM defense against China. By the time

Peking is ready to attack us, we will be able to cope with their missiles in other ways. In a sense, then, the original ABM decision was a bureaucratic budgetary rationalization. The effect of it has been to increase the credibility of the Chinese nuclear threat.

I take a very dim view, incidentally, of Americans trying to put their "Chinese hats" or "Russian hats" on. I do not think we know enough about either mode of thought. Nor do I think that the Chinese can fathom the American psyche. The best we can do—and I think General Griffith did a good job at it— is to try to take some of the objective circumstances that prevail and see if we can interpret the Chinese view of them, but the idea of trying to change our attitudinal approach so that we look at things the way the Chinese do is not only bootless but gets us into a lot of trouble.

WHITING: I do not think that the Administration now believes that the Chinese threat justifies the ABM any more than we do. The Chinese threat has faded significantly in proportion to alternative reasons for the ABM that have been offered by the Nixon Administration. Secretary Laird at one time did speak directly about the Chinese threat, but, by the time the President had reached his decision on March 14, 1969, the number of references to the Chinese had dropped, in proportion to references to the Russians, by about ten to one. I think this is a fair way of phasing it out, and I myself would not belabor the point any longer.

MICHAEL: As I see it, the development of the limited ABM system is partly a matter of experimenting with technique. In the long run, the Chinese threat rests on the fact that they will have ICBMs in the 1970's—that threat is quite real and not totally to be ignored. But what is more, the threat to China's neighbors is immediate. That threat may well imply the necessity of serious consideration of an ABM system in those countries—a point that has never been mentioned. Japan is the largest industrial power in Asia, the third industrial power in the world today, and it will not want to be exposed to this threat unless it can thoroughly rely on U.S. protection. Thus, the ABM system may have, in the long run, a greater importance than simply the defense of the United States.

WHITING: The problem with using a word like "threat" is that it has terribly ominous overtones but no specific content, unless one can construct a situation in which the Chinese could use a nuclear threat to achieve a credible gain that would justify the risks of such a move. Among their risks would be the extermination by us of half of China's population and the elimination of its agricultural base by nuclear weapons and fallout. China could not consider using nuclear weapons lightly or blindly. More specifically, what is the threat to Japan? General Griffith has already said that we cannot expect the development of a significant Chinese airborne and sea-borne offensive capability for another two decades. Apparently then, the Chinese would threaten the Japanese with something other than occupation. Could this be to let the Japanese Communist Party take over? With only 10 per cent of the electorate, this is inconceivable. Would it be to prompt the Japanese to adopt a position of neutrality and force our bases out of Japan? Perhaps. But would that be such a disaster for us? It depends on subsequent events. A neutral Japan would not be a third Asian strategic ally of Communist China or of the Soviet Union.

Nuclear blackmail, in other words, is a term that we have used to frighten ourselves, and, by using it, we have increased nuclear nightmares in Japan, Thailand, and India. We ought to stop educating other people to be as uptight as we are.

BLOOMFIELD: What is the outlook for China's cooperation in arms control negotiations and agreements? Do you believe that if the Soviet Union were still excluded from all world forums and from direct bilateral diplomatic relationships, as it was for seventeen years after its revolution, we would have any of the agreements developed on arms control that we have been able to achieve in the last decade?

GRIFFITH: A credible nuclear capacity might force China into wanting to enter the international community for its own purposes, for its own national security. It might force China to cast off its isolation, which to some extent, of course, is self-created.

As for nuclear arms control agreements, the Chinese will enter discussions similar to those we have had with the Russians when they regard their nuclear system as viable, believe it credible in our eyes, and feel that it will deter us from attacking them. I do not think there will be any successful nuclear arms control arrangements with China until that point is reached. When that point has been reached—and there seems to be general agreement in Washington and probably in Moscow that this will occur in the mid 1970's—the Chinese will be amenable to these discussions.

WHITING: On this question of negotiations and agreements, we have a good deal to learn from the Chinese way of bargaining and politicking among themselves. They prefer the tacit, informal form of bargaining. Lawyers have almost no professional status in China, because the contract is not regarded as something binding on man's behavior.

Since 1950, we have had a tacit renunciation of the use of force in the Taiwan Strait, excluding the offshore islands. Chinese Communists have never flown a reconnaissance aircraft over Taiwan. They have never at any time called what at one time was our bluff: when we were tied down in Korea, we could hardly have fought a continuation of the Chinese civil war in Taiwan as well.

We have pressed for a renunciation of the use of force. We like agreements; we want things spelled out. They will not renounce the use of force in a civil war—to them, that is giving up their proper right.

The same thing is true of border questions: we like to see them nailed down. The Chinese do too; they have made proposals to both the Indians and the Russians in this regard, saying that if their neighbors would admit that the historical treaty that had ceded them the disputed territory was wrong, the Chinese would be willing to continue to recognize those borders, since they existed. In the meantime, they would not use force to try to change them.

If the analogy of China's restraint in the Taiwan Strait, despite the lack of a formal agreement, is projected into the field of arms control, we can have considerably more confidence in China's caution in the nuclear field until such time—which may never come—when the Chinese are ready to sign away what to them are the long desired and finally acquired means of proving through nuclear weapons that they are now "equal." Until then, despite the lack of treaties, we can regard each other's behavior as a tacit means of communication.

COOPER: I agree, but I am troubled by how you actually go about the business of communication. With whom do you communicate? How do you establish meaningful forums? I am not talking about public meetings, in which both of us have to worry about "face," but rather about forums of any kind in which business gets done, however you define business. The Warsaw meetings recently degenerated into situations in which our ambassador listens to the thought of Mao Tse-tung. How do you in fact talk to the Chinese at this time? We can, of course, say what we would like to have done, that we understand that the Chinese have a long and glorious history, that they have problems of "face," that they have lots of difficulties at home. But how do we achieve effective communication with them on arms control or anything else?

BLOOMFIELD: In negotiating with the Chinese, I think we ought to ask ourselves over and over again if we really do appreciate the psychology of the relationship. If we really are aware of "face" considerations and of the fact that race may be one of the most powerful elements in the world today, we must conclude that we cannot accomplish U.S. objectives and expect China to use the back door. China will have to be treated as an equal in diplomacy and arms control negotiations, if we are to succeed in our goals.

MICHAEL: Dealing with Communist China in an informal way, as Allen Whiting said, may be much more meaningful than this belief that we would be able to negotiate with them more successfully if only they were represented formally in such organizations as the United Nations. That belief leads to another problem: the assumption that basically we all think alike and we all want the same thing. If we make that assumption, we misunderstand the goals of Chinese Communism and of Maoism today. We cannot shape the world and the thinking of other people in our image.

We always speak of mainland China as if it were a given entity and as if we knew who would be in power three or five years from now and what the leaders' purposes would be. But today in China there is a power struggle, a very serious power struggle, the outcome of which is undecided, so we do not deal with a unified China, let alone with a China that has the same goals that we have. Furthermore, it is not a matter of communications, it is a matter of purpose.

GRIFFITH: I personally have been in favor of trying to get China into the world community by doing almost anything possible. I am in favor of recognition of China—I would like to see Peking represented in the United Nations. Not that I think its presence would add very much to what goes on there, but, nevertheless, it should sit there. However, I think that Peking will not accept membership in the United Nations so long as Taipei sits on the Security Council. It would not be appropriate for the Chinese to accept representation on such a basis, and I am sure they would not do so. They have laid down certain conditions under which they would enter the United Nations. Still, I wish that we would vote in favor of seating them.

WHITING: On the question of contact with the Chinese, the State Department's announcement in mid-March, 1969, that our ban on travel to China [1] would be extended another six months as a general proposition was, I think, most unfortunate. It has no more justification now than it has had for many, many years. However, within the existing rules, there have been many, many passports validated for journalists—and some writers, scientists, and doctors who have tried to have communication with China. I do not think that the situation of the 1950's has extended into the 1960's. In other words, the break in contact with China that had been imposed in the 1950's by the American government is now more a function of China's unwillingness to let Americans come to China.

QUESTION: [2] Does China have territorial designs on its neighbors? What is the significance of its border disputes in this connection?

COOPER: One can hazard guesses on the basis of feelings and written reports. I do not really think that the Chinese are anxious to conquer Laos or Burma or Vietnam, to make them provinces of China. I am certain that the Chinese have enough problems of their own without trying to conquer India. I am not terribly worried about a large-scale Chinese military thrust into those countries, but trouble-seeking, mischievous acts that upset the existing order are worrisome. In some of these places, it may be high time that the order be upset—but not necessarily by the thought of Mao Tse-tung. There ought to be a better way of doing it.

WHITING: If we look at the border settlements the Chinese

[1] On July 21, 1969, the ban on travel to China was revoked with reference to certain categories of travelers, such as scholars, scientists, and journalists.
[2] Originating from the audience.

have reached during the late 1950's and early 1960's with the Pakistanis, the Afghans, the Nepalese, and the Burmese— and I might add the Outer Mongolians also—in each instance, these treaties have involved generous concessions to formalize borders and have made crystal clear who would be right and who would be wrong.

Chou En-lai went to New Delhi in 1961 and was rebuffed by Prime Minister Nehru in what was apparently an offer to exchange the wasteland of Ladakh for the Northeast Frontier Agency, which the Indians had administered after the British. The Chinese had put a strategic road through Ladakh in violation of Indian claims. The Chinese were willing to waive their so-called claim in the east in return for an Indian waiver in the west. I suspect that the same proposition would be open to any Indian government in the future.

On the border question and on the matter of whom to negotiate with, it is relevant that the British in Hong Kong did find Chinese to negotiate with on their border problems at the height of the Cultural Revolution in 1967 and, after some six weeks of negotiating with the Chinese, worked out those border problems without making any concessions to Peking. Where there is a will, I submit, there is a way.

QUESTION: It is suggested that China has traditionally felt it essential that bordering states be either friendly or neutral. This feeling stems from the former tributary relationships other states maintained with dynastic China. Was this not a factor in China's entry into the Korean War after MacArthur successfully moved north?

WHITING: The Chinese leadership in 1949–50 had a legitimate relationship and shared a common ideology with what they regarded as a legitimate government on their border. To have any sense of their place in Asia, let alone the world, the Chinese had to deny us the option of eliminating that government at will. We were set to eliminate it by invading North Korea and by going right up to the Yalu border. This had nothing to do with the historic traditions of tributary states but everything to do with what modern international politics is all about, and Chinese intervention should be viewed in those terms.

QUESTION: What role do domestic food and population pressures play in China's relations with peripheral states, particularly the rice bowl in Southeast Asia?

WHITING: Many Americans are concerned about the likelihood that Chinese aggression or expansionism will be prompted by population pressure. The Chinese population is not concentrated on the borders where the greatest tension has occurred. China's population is separated from those borders either by the absolutely forbidding Tibetan Himalayan plateaus, the Mongolian Desert, the Sinkiang Desert, or by the northern woods of Manchuria. Topography makes a population explosion in these border areas quite unlikely in the next ten years. It has not occurred in the last hundred years. The Chinese population goes where low capital investment and manpower can raise food—conditions that do not obtain in Tibet, Sinkiang, Outer Mongolia, or Manchuria. Pressure from the Chinese population explosion is not likely to be a relevant factor in Chinese attitudes on border questions.

COOPER: The food and population problem generally is one that we all must worry about over the next decade. The China problem is a part of that.

It seems to me that the problems that the United States, Canada, and the Soviet Union—the "have" nations—will have to face in future years will be dwarfed by the problem the hundreds of millions of people in China and in other parts of the world will have as they try to grope toward not only the problem of escape from famine but that of achieving a better life generally.

When we talk about the future of our relationships with the Soviet Union or with any other country, it seems to me that we are facing a new polarity—not that between the "free world" and the "Communist world," between the Soviet Union and the United States, but the polarity between those of us who have enough and those of us who do not.

As far as the Chinese are concerned, the food problem is one reason for the convulsions of movements like the Great Leap Forward, the Cultural Revolution. They exist with a very, very small cushion between eating and not eating. Whether this has an affect on their foreign policy is not certain. The great rice bowl of Southeast Asia would be available to them, it seems to me, in a sensible world, where people can trade rice for whatever China has to offer. I do not think that China necessarily has to occupy Burma and Thailand in order to get rice. I am not sure that they will be well fed, but at least some of the agricultural surpluses in Southeast Asia could be available to the Chinese.

QUESTION: What are the implications for the United States of a worsening of Sino-Soviet military relations?

WHITING: A number of people in this country are probably saying, "If Dean Rusk and the Russians both say the Chinese are mad, they must be mad." In effect, this is what we are being told by Moscow. But the interesting point is that it was the Russians who in March, 1969, announced a border dispute that had obviously, from both sides' positions, been going on for some time. After announcing it with considerable fanfare, they claimed that the Chinese had started it in order to whip up internal propaganda. But the Russians apparently did not have enough confidence in their case to wait for the Chinese to announce the border clash or to see if they *did* whip it up for internal propaganda reasons. The evidence—not on who fired the first shot, but on who is making the greatest political capital out of this—suggests that it is the Russians who are exerting pressure against the Chinese on the border issue.

In the international Communist world, in Western Europe, and, indeed, in the United States, the image of a triangle is being evoked for U.S.-China-U.S.S.R. relations. Allegedly, if we move toward the Chinese, we must expect the Russians to move away from us. But the triangular relationship in politics is seldom as rigid as it is in geometry. Nor does it follow that one power must be right and the other wrong. This good-guy versus bad-guy dichotomy is not that sound a basis for differentiating among one's adversaries. It is particularly dangerous when one of them tells you that the other is the bad guy. I think that these fallacious assumptions underlie much of our thinking about a possible Sino-Soviet war. We will have to examine them very critically, with special emphasis on our China policy, should such a war come.

MICHAEL: I agree with Allen Whiting. I do not think that the Sino-Soviet border conflict in March, 1969, was a very important one in military terms. There have been border conflicts in this area for quite some time. (Actually, if there is a real war, an island in the Ussuri River would be the most unlikely spot for it to start.) The importance of the clash is that it has been so greatly exploited in propaganda terms.

Both the Soviets and the Chinese have made a great deal of political capital out of it. The question is: Why? I think that the chance that this dispute will escalate into real political conflict is very slight indeed and that, therefore, the question of which side the United States should support is even less real. Why did the Chinese do it? Why did the Soviets do it? There is a possibility of Soviet intervention only if there is conflict in China and if the unity of the Chinese military disintegrates, which is not impossible. For the Chinese, the main thing is to get propaganda value out of the border clash and to try to unify the country and increase lagging support for Mao Tse-tung in a new attempt at re-establishing a Maoist Party. Another reason for the incident might have been the fact that each side was testing the other's prowess and determination.

GRIFFITH: The Chinese in Peking have not been entirely absorbed with the Cultural Revolution. They are perfectly well aware of Soviet conventional capabilities. The Chinese nuclear installations are vulnerable to swift Soviet retaliatory action. Northern Manchuria could be cut off by the Soviets in a week or two. It is fairly good country for the use of mechanized forces, tanks, and so on, since the transportation routes are good. There is also a ring of Soviet airbases around Manchuria, in the Mongolian People's Republic.

I think the people in Peking are realists; they are not going to push these border incidents too far. They might just provoke the Soviets into doing something destructive in a fit of anger. There is not going to be any great furor. These border clashes go on. If two hostile people are on either side of a barbed-wire fence, as was the case along the Sino-Indian border, and both are armed with submachine guns, one day they start cursing each other, the next day they throw rocks, and finally somebody pulls the trigger. I just cannot see any major Sino-Soviet military conflict developing, because I think the Chinese are realists.

COOPER: A major war may be unlikely, but the Sino-Soviet border conflict is a pretty fragile situation, which neither side may be able to control. I doubt that there is much chance of a return to isolationism in this country, but if there is any issue on which we should be isolationist, it is on the issue of a Sino-Soviet war.

QUESTION: Professor Michael said that he did not know whether the PLA could maintain its unity after Mao's death and implied that the PLA is, in fact, a unified force. Professor Walker stated earlier, on the other hand, that the PLA was divided along regional lines, that certain leaders in the PLA were severely antagonistic toward others, and that fighting within the army seems to destroy any idea at all of its unity. Would Professor Michael comment on this?

MICHAEL: I did not mean to give the impression that the Chinese military is clearly united. In fact, there have been very definite signs that it is not. This is one of the reasons why almost anything may happen after Mao's death. There are today quite clear beginnings of regional autonomy. Lin Piao is commanding a sort of inner force—a special force—and is trying to place his own men in key positions in areas that are militarily decisive, particularly in frontier areas in Szechwan, Tibet, Sinkiang, and even in other provinces, but there are indications that central control is limited. While there is no evidence of a split at the moment, there is autonomy, which leads me to regard the situation in China as uncertain.

GRIFFITH: There is no evidence of a deep schism in the People's Liberation Army, and the events of 1966–69 clearly demonstrate, at least to my satisfaction, that the PLA is loyal to the Mao-Lin mainstream faction. Although there is some autonomy in China's regions, I believe that many people in this country have been indulging in wishful thinking about the possibility of internal conflict. They have been hoping ever since the purge of P'eng Teh-huai in 1959 that the PLA would fall apart. It has not fallen apart, and I do not think that it will fall apart. It will remain loyal to the Mao-Lin faction.

WHITING: General Griffith, I think one might differentiate between the PLA as a responsive instrument in the case of external threat and the PLA as an instrument responsive to Mao in domestic issues. I would deny that the PLA has been responsive to Mao's will in internal affairs.

In January, 1967, the PLA was explicitly called upon to take the side of the left, even if the left was in a minority. The army did not do so in many regions of China, however. Instead, by June–July, 1967, a situation had developed in Wuhan—a key city and a main transport artery of China—in which the local PLA regional and divisional commanders both opposed the Maoists from Peking. The Chinese air force had to circle the city for two days dropping Mao's messages because the army would not relay them, and the central authorities had to send units of the East China Sea fleet steaming up the

Yangtze River in a show of strength. When faced with actual civil war within the military system, the rebellious commanders capitulated. They were not punished very severely, it appears, and the local situation there was de-fused. It was not de-fused so easily in other parts of China, however. The damage that has been done to the sense of unity within the military system, and within the army itself, is something that is of importance and relevance for internal Chinese politics—but not for external Chinese policy.

III.

China's Development, Trade, and the World Economy

ROBERT V. ROOSA

The China stage is cut off from Americans by a double curtain. One curtain is lowered by the Chinese themselves; the other is a fire curtain that the United States has put in place to protect Americans from anything that might develop within China. The following observations are from men who, through diligent scholarship or the privileges of another nationality, have had a glance backstage. Their views help clarify whether the United States has more to gain by leaving the fire curtain in place or by raising it.

A universal truth is conveyed in the aphorism that the best way to a man's heart is through his stomach. It is certainly relevant in trying to determine whether there is a heart in mainland China, to probe as deftly as possible into the sources of the nation's livelihood—the progress of the Chinese economy and its trade with the outside world.

WALTER GALENSON

Much of the information on the salient features of Chinese economic development during twenty years of Communist rule is based upon intensive research and analysis by a small group of dedicated economists who have persisted in the face of almost overwhelming odds. During the first decade of their power, the Communists published a relatively small amount of statistical information, which, though of dubious quality, nonetheless provided a basis for analysis, if proper care was taken.[1]

Since 1960, however, quantitative information from China has been embargoed with a thoroughness that is unmatched in modern history. Even in the worst days of Stalinist Russia, some information continued to be published and disseminated abroad. But, in the case of China, not even the most elementary information about population, employment, industrial and agricultural output, trade and commerce, and the

---

[1] These data have been collected, analyzed, and published in N. R. Chen, *Chinese Economic Statistics* (Chicago: Aldine, 1967).

like, has appeared in an open source. It is astounding that an economy can be run at all under such conditions of secrecy, and this policy may explain a good deal about what has happened during the past decade. Any figures pertaining to the years after 1959 are little more than informed guesses, and even those for the previous decade cannot be accepted as hard fact.

It is generally agreed that, during their first three years, the Communists did a good job in cleaning up the debris of civil war and restoring the economy to a semblance of order. By 1952, the gross national product was probably equal to the prewar peak.[2]

In 1953, China embarked upon its first five-year plan. In industry, this period must be accounted a considerable success. From 1953 to 1957, industrial production doubled; the major spurt was in heavy industry, which far outpaced consumer goods production. The program owed a great deal to the willingness of the Soviet Union to sell the Chinese the latest model Soviet equipment, including entire factories, and to Soviet technical assistance.

The weak spot was agriculture. Agricultural stagnation was largely a consequence of insufficient investment. The increase in grain output was small, and, in per capita terms, there was actually a decline, because the population was rapidly increasing at the rate of about 2 per cent a year. From 1952 to 1957, the increase in population was on the order of 70 million.

The emphasis on industry did nothing to help solve the chronic Chinese problem of unemployment and underemployment. From 1952 to 1957, nonagricultural employment grew by less than 2 million. But if one constructs an index with 1952 equal to 100, the national product had risen to 133 by 1957.

[2] Alexander Eckstein has done the major job of analyzing the 1952 national income statistics of China. See *The National Income of Communist China* (New York: Free Press, 1961).

Perhaps in response to this problem, perhaps for ideological reasons as well, the Great Leap Forward strategy was inaugurated in 1958. Emphasis continued to be placed on heavy industry, but an additional aim was full utilization of under-employed rural labor in small industrial and farm projects. The economy made impressive gains in 1958, partly due to a good harvest, but errors in planning and plan implementation led to a serious setback. While industry may have continued to grow until 1960, a severe farm crisis ensued. The national product may have declined by as much as 15 per cent from a peak in 1958 to a trough in 1961.

Recovery began in late 1961 with the adoption of a new policy, which gave priority to agriculture. Beginning in 1962, the national product grew steadily until the onset of the Cultural Revolution, and, in 1965, it may have been about 7 per cent above the 1958 peak.

Industrial production, which dropped sharply in 1961 and even further in 1962, began to move up in 1963. In 1965, it was probably slightly higher than the 1958 level. This was achieved by gradual re-employment of capacity installed before and during the Great Leap rather than by new investment. There were some significant shifts in the relative importance of various branches of industry. The most spectacular development was the rapid growth of the petroleum and chemical fertilizer industries, for which output in 1965 was perhaps five times as great as in 1957.

After the bumper crop of 1958, China experienced three disastrous years. There may have been actual famine in 1961 and 1962. One might have expected a rapid recovery of agriculture with the new policy in 1961, but the neglect of this sector during the previous decade, plus physical and organizational damage inflicted by the Great Leap, made agricultural growth so slow and difficult that Chinese farming may be no more advanced now than in the early 1930's. There have been some achievements: increased use of chemical fertilizers and improved irrigation have contributed to greater land productivity. Cultivated area in 1965, however, is believed to have been below that in 1957, and the output of major crops, except for food grains, had not returned to the levels of the pre-Leap years. In per capita terms, crop production, including grain, was considerably lower in 1965 than in 1957 because of the continued inexorable rise in the population of the country.

The Cultural Revolution undoubtedly affected the economy adversely, but it is difficult to determine by how much. The available evidence indicates that the damage was not as great as the dislocations caused by the Great Leap and that the impact on agriculture was much less than on industry and transport. An informed guess might place the 1968 national product somewhere in the vicinity of the 1965 level, 50 to 60 per cent above that of 1952. This would give a somewhat lower rate of growth than Professor Eckstein indicates later in this chapter.

How does China's rate of growth compare with that of India? Some very rough calculations would indicate that, on the basis of the entire planning periods in India and in China since 1952, the average rate of growth of the two countries for this entire period has been about the same. It is a tortoise and hare situation. The Chinese were off to a rapid start in 1952, peaked out in the Great Leap Forward, dropped disastrously in a great downward cycle, moved up again during the Cultural Revolution, and then dropped again. The Indians, with a much less spectacular type of development program, moved up rather slowly but fairly steadily, allowing for certain fluctuations in the harvest, and have come out at about the same place as the Chinese.

Chinese economic development since 1949 has had both its positive and negative aspects. An industrial base capable of supporting a nuclear capacity and producing a wide variety of industrial goods has been established, but agriculture has not kept up with population growth, and this remains a serious problem for the regime.

For the future, the following are the essential ingredients of a national, optimal development policy:

1. First and most important, the rate of population growth must be reduced. Nothing would contribute more to reducing the present burden on the economy. A heavy investment in birth control is called for. There is some indication that, at least until 1965, the Communist leaders were beginning to effectuate this policy.

2. Next in importance is a comprehensive program to raise agricultural productivity. This can be done not by pushing the long-suffering Chinese peasant into ever new forms of organization but only by the greater use of chemical fertilizers, improved seed, and pesticides. Were China to open its doors and enter the world economy, crop specialization along the lines dictated by comparative advantage would be an effective means of progress. With its huge manpower resources, China could become the world's supplier of labor-intensive agricultural goods.

3. In the industrial sector, China should be producing such labor-intensive goods as clothing, textiles, and electronic and optical goods. Chinese comparative advantage lies elsewhere than in automobiles, steel, shipbuilding, and heavy machinery.

4. The handicraft industries, which are labor-intensive by definition, have particularly good prospects. The Communists have preserved the traditional crafts but have not given sufficient attention to design, quality standards, and marketing organization. China could put art goods and domestic wares in millions of homes the world over.

5. All of this hinges upon a great expansion of foreign trade. Western Europe and the United States, along with Japan, are the logical suppliers of the capital goods China needs badly. But these areas, in turn, must be prepared to absorb

the products of labor-intensive industry that China can supply cheaply.

This is an optimal program, but it is doubtful that it will be effectuated. The more extreme Maoists appear to be calling for a new Great Leap, a return to break-neck industrialization via the capital-intensive route. Autarky, rather than international trade, is consonant with traditional Chinese attitudes toward the outside world. A "Great Power" complex, with its military requirements, may induce the Communist leadership to go all out for heavy industry. Whatever its contribution to modernization and growth, this policy would mean for the Chinese people even greater hardships in the future than they have borne in the past.

ALEXANDER ECKSTEIN

The central facts about the Chinese economy today are that it is poor, underdeveloped, technically backward, and trying to industrialize rapidly. In essence, it is a small economy in a vast country. Thus, a country with roughly the same territory as the United States and with a population three and a half times as large is sustained by an economy that in total size is about one-tenth that of the United States. As a result, national income per capita is about $100 in China as compared to about $1,000 in Japan, $2,000 in the Soviet Union, and $4,500 in the United States.

How rapidly has this backward economy been moving since the Communist regime came to power and what are its development prospects over the next decade? Allowing for serious deficiencies in the available data, it would seem that China's national income has perhaps risen by 75 per cent between 1952 and 1969. This would indicate a rate of growth of about 4 per cent, which is faster than that of India but slower than that of the most rapidly growing countries of the underdeveloped world. It is also slower than the postwar growth rates of Japan and the Soviet Union but somewhat above those for the United States.

In China, as in all developing countries, the process of economic growth and industrialization has been painful. Riding the crest of a great victory on the one hand and having available unutilized or underutilized labor and plant capacity on the other, the new regime gained a great deal of political and economic momentum and thus was able to push the economy rapidly forward. Therefore, the first decade of Communist rule did indeed turn out to be "ten great years" [1] for the economy.

As the economy moved rapidly forward during these years, unemployed labor and plant capacity became more fully employed, and, as a result, increasing strains, imbalances, supply bottlenecks, and shortages of all kinds appeared. These tendencies were greatly aggravated by the very sluggish advance in agriculture and the failure of agriculture to keep pace with industrial development.

In these terms, the Great Leap Forward (1958–60) can be viewed as a supreme effort to eliminate these development bottlenecks and to launch the economy on a path of self-sustaining growth. Unfortunately for the Chinese Communists, this effort failed—essentially because they tried to do too much too fast. It also failed because the leadership was still hoping to cope with the problem of agricultural development —not by investing more in agriculture, not by applying more chemical fertilizer and modern farm equipment, but by still relying on traditional methods.

The Great Leap led to a profound agricultural and economic crisis, which disrupted China's economic advance. Under the impact of this great disaster, policy-makers finally assigned a

[1] A term the Chinese Communists have applied to their first ten years of rule on the mainland.

higher priority to agricultural development so that the country could begin to recover from this deep depression. Recovery and new development after 1962 were slowed down between 1966 and 1968 because of the negative economic effects of the Cultural Revolution.

What has been witnessed in China during the past two decades is a highly fluctuating and uneven pattern of development. Amidst the ups and downs, and on the basis of these two decades of experience, it would seem that the economy at its present stage of development could at best support a trend rate of national income growth of from 4 to 5 per cent per year. Whether in fact such a rate can be attained during the next decade will depend on a number of imponderables, of which political factors in general and economic policy factors in particular may be most important.

As one looks ahead, the greatest element of uncertainty is the longevity and political durability of Mao. China's economic prospects are likely to be much more promising once Mao passes from the scene. It would seem that Mao and his supporters consider the permanence of the revolution, the maintenance of a revolutionary dynamic, and the attainment of "pure" socialism as their primary goals. In their view, industrialization must serve as the handmaiden of this process. Therefore, if the requirements of industrialization dictate compromise with these goals, industrialization rather than the pursuit of socialism must be sacrificed.

Leaving aside these policy imponderables, the country's economy is bound to face many problems during the next decade. Ultimately, the principal and most crucial barriers to industrialization in China are the same as in all other underdeveloped countries: scarcity of capital and scarcity of skills, as evidenced by acute shortages of scientific, engineering, and technical manpower.

Whether and to what extent these development barriers can be overcome will depend in large degree upon the sophistication and effectiveness of the economic planning mechanism. If the past is any guide in this respect, the prospects are not very encouraging. However, once Mao disappears, and if the succession struggle can be resolved so that a certain measure of political stability is attained, it will be much easier to formulate and implement economic policies conducive to development. Even if this occurs, and the Chinese economy grows at an average rate of from 4 to 5 per cent over the next decade, China's national product per head in 1980 would at best be about $120. In effect, it would be still very, very far below that of Japan and the Soviet Union today.

Could this picture be modified if China were to become more closely integrated into the world trading system? The tentative first answer to that question might be perhaps, to some extent. In analyzing this problem, it must be remembered that the same general factors that circumscribe the pace of China's economic development also constrain its foreign-trade capacity. This situation could be markedly altered only if it were possible to import capital on a large scale. Under such circumstances, the country's imports would not need to be limited by exports, and import surpluses could be maintained and utilized for domestic development and for increasing export capacity.

What role has foreign trade played in China's development and what place has China occupied in the world trading system? Foreign trade represents a small but very important segment of the Chinese economy. Exports or imports constitute only about 3 to 5 per cent of the gross national product. However, these imports played a decisive role in the 1950's in fostering rapid industrialization through purchases of machinery, equipment, and complete plants. In the 1960's, on the other hand, imports were crucial in maintaining economic and political stability, inasmuch as grain supplies from abroad constituted a marginally decisive increment to domestic food supplies.

Just as China's foreign trade was small in relation to the country's gross national product, it was even smaller in relation to total world trade. Mainland China's foreign trade expanded very rapidly during the 1950's. It doubled between 1952 and 1959 but then declined drastically under the impact of the economic crisis. Foreign trade also began to recover in 1962 and, by 1966, somewhat exceeded the former peak level (1959). It has declined slightly since 1966, due to the impact of the Cultural Revolution.

At peak levels, China's imports and exports have totaled approximately $2 billion to $2.4 billion. This means that its foreign trade is smaller than that of most West European countries.

The country's trading patterns have changed drastically in the 1960's, as compared with the 1950's. Until 1955, China maintained a trade deficit, which was largely financed by Soviet loans. Between 1955 and 1966, however, even including the crisis years, the country maintained a trade surplus, which was used to amortize the Soviet credits and later to rebuild foreign-exchange reserves. This relationship has been reversed once again in the last two years, with the economic problems imposed by the Cultural Revolution leading to some decline in exports without a corresponding decline in imports.

The most dramatic shifts in China's trading patterns took place in the direction of trade. During the 1950's, about 40 to 60 per cent of commercial interchange was with the Soviet Union and another 15 to 20 per cent was with Eastern Europe. Trade with the non-Communist world fluctuated between 20 and 35 per cent. After the Sino-Soviet break, this situation was sharply reversed. Thus, in 1967, trade with the Soviet Union declined to 2 per cent and with East Europe to 6 per cent of China's total trade. As a result, the non-Communist world's trade with China increased not only in relative but in absolute terms as well. China's total trade turnover with non-Communist countries rose from about $1.5 billion in

1958 to about $3.4 billion in 1967. The principal beneficiaries of this shift were Japan, Hong Kong, Canada, Australia, and Germany.

Is this process of rapid trade expansion likely to continue during the next decade? In answering this question, one must bear in mind that, during the last ten years, the growth of China's trade with these countries was largely due to a redirection of its trade from Communist to non-Communist partners. Since trade with the Soviet Union and Eastern Europe has already dwindled to very small proportions, there is very little room left for further shifts. The growth from now on will necessarily depend on China's capacity to increase its total trade, that is, its capacity to increase exports and absorb imports.

In the 1950's, China imported primarily industrial raw materials and capital goods. In the 1960's, the country became a large-scale grain importer. In the early part of the decade, grain virtually displaced machinery, equipment, and complete plant imports. In recent years, grain imports have been declining somewhat, while industrial raw materials and capital goods have again been gaining in importance. This trend may be expected to continue at least over the next five years. Specifically, China is likely to remain a significant market for food grains, chemical fertilizer, certain types of metals, and a wide range of machinery products.

There has been a much less pronounced change on the export side. Throughout the past two decades, the principal exports have been foodstuffs, raw materials of agricultural origin, and cotton textiles. At the same time, textiles have been continuously gaining in relative importance, as have manufactured consumer goods such as bicycles and fountain pens.

Barring the import of large quantities of capital, China's import possibilities are likely to be determined by exports. This means that the country's foreign trade will largely depend on the economy's ability to supply increasing exports drawn mostly from agriculture and the manufacture of consumer goods. It will also naturally depend on China's ability to find markets for these products.

Were one to assume that exports would grow at the same rate as previously assumed for the gross national product, China's foreign trade could be expected to increase by about 40 per cent in the next ten years. This would mean, on the average, an annual addition of $80 to $100 million to exports and imports.

Some of these additional exports may be expected to be marketed in the industrialized countries. This could be the case for soybeans and their products and for other agricultural goods. On the other hand, textiles and other manufactured consumer goods will have to find their markets in underdeveloped countries where they are likely to encounter stiff competition from domestic producers and from exporters among other underdeveloped or semi-industrialized countries. In contrast, China is not likely to encounter many difficulties in obtaining the import goods required by its consumers and producers, the United States embargo notwithstanding.

In summary then, under the most optimistic assumptions, Communist China may be expected to be a $100 billion economy by 1980, with a per capita income of about $120. Thus, China's economic capabilities are likely to remain highly limited. Viewed in this perspective, its foreign trade may be expected to increase gradually. In spite of its hundreds of millions of potential customers, as long as the country remains poor, China will constitute a modest but not insignificant export market.

Since the United States today is the only country in the world, or at least certainly the only major trading nation in the world, that maintains a virtually complete embargo on all trading transactions—goods and payments, exports and imports—with China, we are precluded from participation in this

Chinese market, while the economic effect of the embargo is negligible, because China can import from European countries all the goods it wants, with the exception of strategic materials on the U.S. embargo list.

Politically, the embargo stands as a symbol of the continuing and unalterable determination of the United States to isolate China. That is its only practical political effect. It has a psychological effect also in that it gives the American public and the American Congress the illusion that, in some sense, the United States is hurting China, while, in fact, the embargo has no practical effect in terms of retarding China's economic development.

The economic effect is negative from America's point of view in that this embargo denies U.S. business enterprises access to the mainland Chinese market. Through our foreign asset control regulations, these trade restrictions reach beyond the boundaries of the United States. As a result, any business enterprise abroad that is a subsidiary of an American corporation or has substantial American financial investment is subject to the same embargo regulations as prevail in the United States. Moreover, if a British enterprise, for instance, exports to China certain goods it has produced with American components that are on the U.S. embargo list, it is placed on the U.S. blacklist. This, in turn, will seriously jeopardize its ability to export to the United States.

JOHN M. KESWICK

It is useful to look at trade as affected by politics and the degree of recognition accorded to China. The details of Russian, British, and Japanese trade with China must be discussed with some reserve because statistics on China's foreign trade are inadequate for our purposes. The best sources of knowledge on China trade are the Communist and non-Communist countries that trade with China. If their data are combined, the results are better than trying to extract figures from Chinese publications. Over the years, some indicative trends have been established.

The United Kingdom recognized China in a limited manner in 1949 and, during the next few years, began to make some advance in trading. It was possible to go to Peking and talk business with the officials of the Peking government. Since the Cultural Revolution, this has virtually come to an end.

The Russians have a long history of diplomatic relations with China. They have long had an exchange of ambassadors and, during the first decade of the Chinese Communist revolution, Russian planners and Russian machines poured into China in great quantities. The advantage and the help given to China's economy by Russia was huge indeed. The two countries pledged everlasting friendship, and streets and buildings in both countries were named after Sino-Soviet amity. Then, alas, political quarrels started, and today China's trade and intercourse with Russia have reached a low ebb. In fact, these two countries are at daggers drawn.

Since the war, Japan has not exchanged ambassadors or had official diplomatic relations with China, but trade has flourished. Pressures from America and Taiwan have tended to restrain Japan's trade with China, but trade has continued and expanded. It has had its setbacks, such as the famous Yoshida letter to Chiang Kai-shek promising stringent credit restrictions on Japan's trade with China. That reduced trade possibilities considerably, but trade did develop, in spite of the lack of diplomatic relations and in spite of the American presence around Japan and American influence on Japan's policies.

Other countries, such as Holland, have had difficulties when their diplomatic staff has become involved in fracases of various kinds. Politics intrudes constantly and makes the expansion of trade extremely uncertain. On the other hand, the British have done surprisingly well in spite of the difficulties. In the past ten years, they have been in and out of the political dog house with China quite frequently and are in it at the moment, due to Hong Kong and the attitude of Peking toward Hong Kong.

In 1964, there was a British engineering trade exhibition in Peking; I was the president of that and I was very enthusiastic at the reception we received. I felt that our chances of expanding our exports to China were very great, and I made a rash prognostication at that time in Peking that Sino-British trade would increase by 50 per cent. In fact, it did a good deal better. In 1964, British total trade with China was $119 million. In 1965, it went up to $156 million, in 1966, to $188

million, and, in 1967, it was about $190 million. Then, follow-
ing the 1967 riots and troubles over Hong Kong and other
effects of the Cultural Revolution, trade began to dip. The
following table gives an export-import breakdown in millions
of dollars for those years:[1]

	1964	1965	1966	1967	1968
U.K. exports to China	49.9	72.3	93.6	108.0	68.3
U.K. imports from China	68.9	83.2	94.7	81.6	82.3
Total	118.8	155.5	188.3	189.6	150.6

I have tried to point out how politics and trade go hand
in hand. On the other hand, extraordinary anomalies take
place. In 1968 and 1969, exports from England could have
been expected to drop, owing to the situation in Hong Kong.
However, British export figures for January–February, 1969,
were about twice the corresponding figures for 1968. Why
should British trade be rising in 1969? The answer lies with
the Chinese. When they want to buy something, they go to
the market to buy it, and, if they feel that they must have a
commodity or a machine, they seem to have little difficulty in
achieving their requirements. At the moment, minerals, such
as copper, platinum, and diamonds, have been cheaper in the
United Kingdom than they are on the continent of Europe
or in Africa, and the Chinese bought pretty heavily in the first
two months of 1969 in London.

The problems and hazards of trade with China are not one-
sided. England imposes quotas on imports from China, which
aggravate the Chinese a great deal and are an impediment to
trade. The reason for the import quotas is to protect British
industries. Similarly, the United Kingdom adheres firmly to

[1] *Sources:* 1964 and 1965, *Far Eastern Economic Review Yearbook 1967*
(Hong Kong: Far Eastern Economic Review, Ltd., 1966), p. 157; 1966 and
1967, *Far Eastern Economic Review Yearbook 1969* (Hong Kong: Far Eastern
Economic Review, Ltd., 1968), p. 148; 1968, P. H. M. Jones, "Trade Marks
Time," *Far Eastern Economic Review*, 40 (October 2, 1969), p. 45.

the COCOM Agreements in Paris, which are an instrument of embargo.[2] Unlike the U.S. embargo, which is total, the CO-COM embargo is placed only on a list of strategic goods, as internationally defined. These two impediments, the quota system and the COCOM Agreements, are difficult hurdles for British traders and others to leap. It is extraordinary that so many of the items the Chinese want to buy are on the COCOM list. Some of the world's countries observe it more strictly than others.

In China today, it is impossible to forecast what will happen, except that one is certain to encounter politics as soon as one steps inside the country. A call on the Bank of China or one of the great trading corporations or machinery corporations results in a courteous greeting and a cup of tea and anywhere from five to ten minutes of political indoctrination as well before business begins. Then, however, if official trading corporations want to buy something or want to sell something, the trading process is relatively easy, though often slow. Before an agreement is reached, a complicated transaction will entail a prolonged argument and discussion, which are often interrupted when the chief negotiator calls a halt for half an hour while he and his men go off to have a special political meeting.

[2] The COCOM Agreements were originally established by the coordinating committee of the United Nations in 1950. Under the agreements, the NATO countries and Japan have placed an embargo on the shipment of an extensive list of goods to China, North Korea, and the Communist countries of Europe.

ALVIN HAMILTON

It is almost impossible to separate trade from politics when dealing with the Chinese. The Chinese say they are willing to trade with any nation that will trade with them. They say that this policy is not dependent on recognition or admission to the United Nations. However, as Professor Alexander Eckstein has pointed out in his most recent book,[1] in about 1960 the external trade of China began to shift away from the Communist nations and move toward other nations. This shift may have been because the Western world had what the Chinese wanted, but its occurrence is more likely due to the break in Sino-Soviet relations.

The fact that the United Kingdom and France have diplomatic relations with China has not meant that their nationals get a friendly reception from Chinese officials, who always remind a visitor who the imperialists of the nineteenth century

---

[1] Alexander Eckstein, *Communist China's Economic Growth and Foreign Trade* (New York: McGraw-Hill, 1966).

were. Even the tourists who go there on private business are always shown the signs or the places where the signs used to be that said "Dogs and Chinese not allowed." The exception to this frigid reception is the Scot, who for some reason is not classified as English and seems welcome everywhere.

The Japanese are vividly remembered for their activities in China during the long hostilities of the Sino-Japanese War. The Chinese differentiate between Indians and Pakistanis. As for the Russians, they are described as simply "worse than the English."

The official Chinese attitude toward Americans and Canadians seems to be that the people are all right but that both political parties in both countries are the tools of big business. And big business in the Chinese official mind is the military-economic relationship, which to them adds up to "aggression for profit."

It is on this point that their Prime Minister Chou En-lai and I had a difference of opinion. I said that, in my observation of American and Canadian business, most businessmen were a timid lot overwhelmed by the size and power of big government. Only the steel companies, the automobile companies, and the independent oil producers had ever stood up to the American government in recent years and, as far as I had been able to gather, only the oil producers had gotten away with it.

Furthermore, I emphasized that business was not monolithic and that of all people Chou En-lai should be the last person to deride American business. By the very nature of the system under which they operate, businessmen in the United States, I told him, could not stand idly by and watch a market of 700 million—soon to be 1 billion people—be picked up by lesser powers like Canada and Australia who did not deny to their citizens the right to trade with anybody on grounds of color or politics. I boldly predicted that in five years Americans would be trading with the Chinese.

His response was pretty quick. In essence, it was that my portrayal of American business was to him "very interesting," but he thought that I was optimistic in making the five-year estimate. That discussion took place in March, 1964.

Canadians have a special place in the Chinese mind. Canadians are looked on as allies of the United States, with all the implications thereof. The Chinese do not blame Canada particularly, but they watch it carefully to see how many times it acts on its own. They have made a national hero of Canadian Dr. Norman Bethune, who died on the battlefield looking after wounded Communist soldiers. And more recently, when the Chinese parted company with the Russians, it was the Canadians who first approached them with an offer to sell wheat at a time when they needed it and when they thought that they were isolated from the rest of the world. The Chinese character is strong on gratitude.

Without understanding the relationship between politics and trade, there can be little progress in trade. Part of the politics is foreign policy. At the risk of oversimplification, the objectives of Chinese foreign policy can be summarized as follows:

1. To recover lost territories
2. To establish some sort of Chinese Monroe Doctrine
3. To take over the leadership of the Communist international movement

On the first point, the Chinese seem happy with the new boundaries with India and Pakistan. Their outstanding objectives still to be realized are the recovery of Taiwan and the big territory opposite Sinkiang. Therefore, on this score, the Russians, not the Americans, are their major enemy. On the second point, their demonstrated sensitivity regarding Korea and Vietnam indicates that the close military containment of their country by the Americans makes the United States their major enemy. On the third point, the leadership of the Communist world, their only enemy is Russia. Thus, the Russians are China's main opponents, and the Chinese leaders wonder why the United States takes so long to understand this. Naturally, they are afraid of a Russian-American alliance.

The Chinese have stated many times that they will trade with anybody who will trade with them—even without recognition. This is evident in their trade with Australia and Canada. In the case of the United States, they take delight in pointing out that the United States has laws and regulations that prohibit its nationals from trading with them. They used to point out that the U.S. Government would not allow Americans to visit China. When Washington expressed its willingness to allow professional people and academics to go, they backed off this criticism and resorted to criticism of the trade restrictions.

What is China's real attitude toward trade? The Chinese know that their national economic growth rate is slow, probably about 2 per cent on a per capita basis. They must decide how much of their economic resources should go to provide a military posture against the Russians and the Americans and how much can be put into improving development capital for domestic purposes.

The Chinese are certainly aware of the tremendous pressure of the consumer for more goods. Chinese high school and university students are quite outspoken in their desire to get some of this world's goods in their lifetime. The Chinese also know that trade between nations makes faster growth possible. Their trade figures in the last ten years prove their desire to move up in the field of world trade, to improve their own domestic growth.

When I was there in 1964, they told me that their priorities for imports were (1) farm machinery, (2) chemical fertilizers, (3) newsprint, (4) certain metals or minerals, and (5) lumber (if they can ever afford it).

As for exports, they know they are a rich agricultural country with an agricultural surplus and that much of their export earnings will therefore have to come from the export of food.

They are able to produce low-grade steel, which will not sell in the Western world but will sell in the underdeveloped nations, and they produce a rather good quality of certain machine tools, bathroom equipment, and, of course, handicrafts, which seem to offer fascinating possibilities.

Even at a 2 per cent per capita growth rate, the potential market each year for such a large number of people is more than sizable. If the Chinese could reduce the cost of maintaining a military posture against the United States and make those funds available for capital and consumer goods, their growth rate would tend to increase. This, in turn, would make for an even better market.

There are problems in trading with China. Internally, the highway system is city-oriented. The railway system is efficient insofar as it has capacity. China has not reached the international level in grading, packaging, and storing. The Chinese require a long time to plan production and a long time to get into production. Against this, there is high quality craftsmanship, which promises well for them in the future.

Canada knows that it is caught in the North American industrial web. Companies that are subsidiaries of American corporations cannot enter the China trade, because the officers of their parent company would be prosecuted under American law. In addition, Canadian companies with large markets in the United States fear that there will be a reaction against their goods in the United States if they follow Canadian government policy and trade with China.

As a Canadian, I try to get Canadians to produce what the Chinese need and take advantage of the lead that we have over the United States, but, as a citizen of the world, I am interested in seeing the strain between the Chinese and the Americans lessened. While Canadians may not get as much of the trade if the United States trades with China, the reduced risk of war will benefit everyone.

Even if the American government is persuaded to reduce

the trade restrictions that are now imposed on trade with China, there will be no sudden increase in trade between the United States and China. Individual American businessmen will have to learn how to deal with the Chinese as individuals. The Chinese know that they are the most cultured people in the world and that the rest of us are barbarians, and any businessman who thinks that he can fly in one day and conduct business and have a reservation out the next is not going to do much business in China. Cultured people have a cup of tea before discussions start and before they depart. Businessmen are going to have to learn to listen to propaganda and to appreciate the works of a 5,000-year-old culture as well as occasionally the thought of Mao Tse-tung.

FREDERICK S. BEEBE

In response to a request for comments on the state of the
Chinese economy, the *Newsweek* and *Washington Post*
bureaus in Tokyo, Hong Kong, London, Paris, Bonn, Ottawa,
New York, Washington, and Los Angeles have expressed an
extraordinary unanimity with the view of the Chinese economy
that has been offered by professors Eckstein and Galenson.
That view can be briefly summarized by quoting from some
comments made by the chief of the *Washington Post* bureau
in Hong Kong, Stanley Karnow. He is one of the real China
hands in journalism and has spent many years in Hong Kong
and other countries in Asia. He said:

> Any discussion of China's economic prospects must necessarily
> start from the premise that China is an overpopulated, under-
> developed country with no plausible expectations of registering
> dramatic growth in the foreseeable future. It is highly unlikely
> that China will offer attractive commercial opportunities in the
> years ahead, at least on a national scale. The great dream of mil-
> lions of Chinese customers that was popularized in the 1930's in

many quarters is very much a mirage. Indeed, it is clear that the countries trading with China at present are not really reaping important benefits in relation to their total commerce.

Just one final summary thought looking to the future: It is not far-fetched to speculate that, after Mao's death, China will see the emergence of a more pragmatic, modern leadership aware of their country's tremendous limitations and perhaps receptive to what they can gain from the world beyond the Middle Kingdom. Nor is it outlandish to suppose that these leaders might even regard the United States as a source of the technological assistance they will need to develop China. This does not mean that China will be the El Dorado of the Columbus dream. It could more plausibly be a less fractious, underdeveloped country, willing to seek help through trade and credits and, in the process, to establish a more reasonable link with international society.

That comment summarizes a great deal of material that came in from around the world.

One striking point, which puts into perspective the situation as these correspondents see it, is the observation that China's estimated international trade in 1967 was somewhat less than that of Denmark.

All this does not mean, however, that the United States should be unconcerned about the future of the Chinese economy or of its economic relations with China or indeed about the steps that could be taken to improve those relations. Clearly, China, with all its economic difficulties, has enormous capacities to take economic steps that are of really immeasurable importance to the United States. Such capacities include the demonstrated ability of the Chinese to develop nuclear capability and apparently to develop missiles capable of delivering the nuclear warheads that they have developed. This is a tremendous technological feat, and any country capable of achieving this—particularly the missile development they apparently are able to achieve—is not one that can be ignored nor is it one that the United States can afford to deal with in terms of old clichés and old ideological concepts.

Most encouraging in this regard is the fact that the American people are no longer thinking in terms of the old kind of ideological responses that have infected U.S. public opinion about China for the last fifteen to twenty years. As the recent Gallup poll printed below indicates, the United States is coming to a point where people are going to be willing to examine American relations with China in the spirit of a healthy desire to advance American foreign policy. It should be a skeptical examination and it should not contemplate that there will be a great leap forward in U.S.-China relations. But given that as a background attitude, there is great reason to be optimistic about the capacity of the United States and the willingness of the U.S. Government and opinion leaders realistically to approach the whole problem of China, China's economy, and Sino-American trade in a healthy and constructive fashion.

Gallup Poll *

In October, 1966, and February, 1969, the Gallup poll posed the following question: "Do you think Communist China should or should not be admitted as a member of the United Nations?" The responses were as follows:

	February, 1969			October, 1966		
	Should	Should not	No opinion	Should	Should not	No opinion
	%	%	%	%	%	%
National	33	54	13	25	56	19
Sex						
Men	39	52	9			
Women	27	56	17			
Race						
White	33	55	12			

*Reprinted by permission of The Gallup Organization, Inc. The 1966 poll, as published, provides no breakdown by population group. X—no information available.

	February, 1969			October, 1966		
	Should	Should not	No opinion	Should	Should not	No opinion
	%	%	%	%	%	%
Non-white	X	X	X			
Education						
College	49	45	6			
High school	31	57	12			
Grade school	21	57	22			
Occupation						
Prof. & bus.	41	53	6			
White collar	30	58	12			
Farmers	31	53	16			
Manual	30	55	15			
Age						
21–29 years	45	46	9			
30–49 years	33	56	11			
50 & over	27	56	17			
Religion						
Protestant	28	58	14			
Catholic	39	50	11			
Jewish	X	X	X			
Politics						
Republican	32	55	13			
Democrat	30	55	15			
Independent	39	52	9			
Region						
East	37	50	13			
Midwest	33	54	13			
South	23	60	17			
West	40	52	8			
Income						
$10,000 & over	41	52	7			
$ 7,000 & over	40	52	8			
$ 5,000–$6,999	32	57	11			
$ 3,000–$4,999	23	60	17			
Under $3,000	21	53	26			
Community size						
1,000,000 & over	38	52	10			
500,000 & over	38	51	11			

| | February, 1969 | | | | October, 1966 | | |
| | Should | Should not | No opinion | | Should | Should not | No opinion |
	%	%	%		%	%	%
50,000–499,999	37	50	13				
2,500–49,999	23	62	15				
Under 2,500, rural	29	56	15				

LUKE T. LEE

When the news came that Peking had asked for a resumption of ambassadorial talks in Warsaw after President Nixon's election, it occurred to me that, sooner or later, one of the topics of the talks would be trade. Since mainland China has been a large consumer of wheat during the last few years from Canada, Australia, France, and Argentina, wheat should logically be an important item of Sino-American trade. However, how would U.S. public opinion regard the question of sales of U.S. wheat to China? One aspect of this question was how wheat growers themselves would feel about the question and, particularly, wheat growers in such relatively conservative states as Nebraska and Wyoming. There was a nagging doubt as to whether the Nebraskan wheat growers would be willing to sell wheat to mainland China, in view of the popular assumption that public opinion in this country is strongly opposed to trade with mainland China.

In order to find an answer to this question, I broached the subject of canvassing wheat growers' attitudes toward wheat

sales to China to my colleagues in the University of Nebraska
Agricultural School, whose faculty includes Dr. Clifford Hardin, now on leave and serving as Secretary of Agriculture. Together, we drew up a questionnaire and persuaded the
Nebraska-Wyoming Wheat Growers' Association to conduct
a poll among its members. We chose the December, 1968,
meeting of the Association held in Ogallala, Nebraska, as the
occasion for conducting the poll. Members were not warned
about the poll before the meeting, and, according to the Association Secretary, the turn-out for the meeting was a representative one. The questionnaire read:

> In view of [then] President-elect Nixon's agreement to hold Ambassadorial talks with Peking [in] February [1969], and in view
> of continued wheat sales to mainland China by our close allies—
> Canada and Australia—although neither has recognized its government, do you, as wheat growers, think the United States
> should sell wheat to mainland China?
>
> Yes _____
> No _____
>
> Please comment if you wish:
>
> (a) Would you suggest any special conditions or restrictions
> under which the wheat should be sold, as for example: Should we
> sell it for cash or under short- or long-term loans?
>
> (b) Other comments.

Out of 41 members who responded to this questionnaire
at the meeting, 39 voted "Yes" and only 2 voted "No". More
than 95 per cent were in favor of selling wheat to China.

It is interesting to note some of the comments made about
the conditions or restrictions under which wheat should be sold
to China. Two would sell wheat under Public Law 480 (that
is, sales of surplus wheat to underdeveloped countries in return
for payment in the local unconvertible currency); 1, not under
Public Law 480; 28, for cash; 2, under long-term credit; 1, for
gold only; and 1, under the prevailing market conditions.

One respondent justified wheat sales to China on the ground that food is the best weapon for peace; another said China would get wheat from other countries anyway; three would want to use wheat sales to improve relations with China; and one said we should sell to the Chinese anything they could eat, drink, or smoke. Of the two respondents who opposed selling wheat to China, one said he opposed such sales because China might later destroy the United States, and the other had no comment.

Despite the favorable responses to the sale of wheat to mainland China, it should be stressed that this survey was far from complete or perfect, and that I am not a professional pollster. Nevertheless, the survey does raise serious questions as to the validity of the prevailing assumption that public opinion in this country is strongly opposed to trading with mainland China. The result of the survey is more significant since Nebraska is a conservative Republican state and gave Nixon the largest percentile vote during the last election. Since those opposing trade with China often use public opinion as justification, it may be time to have a systematic and in-depth survey of public opinion on this issue. Hopefully, this rudimentary survey will lead to future comprehensive and systematic surveys.

Postscript

Responding to my suggestion that more comprehensive and systematic surveys be conducted on possible trade with China, John Cowles, Chairman of *The Minneapolis Star and Tribune*, graciously obliged by sponsoring such a poll in Minnesota. The results [1] support my view by showing that Minnesotans of different educational levels and geographical districts are by no means strongly opposed to trade with mainland China.

---

[1] *The Minneapolis Tribune*, June 4, 1969. © 1969 Minneapolis Star and Tribune Company. Reprinted by permission of the publisher.

This in-depth survey is reproduced not only because of its important revelations, but also with a view to encouraging the taking of similar surveys in different states.

Minnesotans are evenly divided over whether there should be trade between the United States and Communist China.

In a statewide survey by The Minneapolis Tribune's Minnesota Poll, 44 per cent said it would be a good idea to sell wheat and other agricultural products to mainland China. Forty-six per cent said it would be a poor idea. Ten per cent were undecided.

People are slightly more resistant to having American business firms trade with the Chinese on the mainland, excluding materials of war: 40 per cent favored such trade and 51 per cent were opposed . . .

The survey was conducted this spring [1969] among a balanced sampling of 594 voting-age men and women living in cities, villages, and farm areas in every congressional district of Minnesota. Seventy of the people interviewed were farm men and women. These are the questions asked and the replies received:

"Do you think Communist China should or should not be admitted to the United Nations?"

	All adults	Men	Women
Should be admitted	37%	43%	32%
Should not	55	50	60
No opinion	8	7	8
	100%	100%	100%

"Do you think it would be a good idea or poor if the United States were to sell wheat and other agricultural products to mainland China?"

	All adults	Men	Women
Good idea	44%	51%	38%
Poor idea	46	42	50
No opinion	10	7	12
	100%	100%	100%

"*Except for war materials, would you favor or oppose allowing American business firms to carry on trade with firms in mainland China?*"

	All adults	Men	Women
Favor	40%	46%	35%
Oppose	51	48	54
No opinion	9	6	11
	100%	100%	100%

The following table shows how opinions vary from question to question among certain types of Minnesotans. The first line repeats the finding that, among all Minnesotans, 37 per cent think Communist China should be admitted to the United Nations, that 44 per cent think agricultural trade is a good idea, and that 40 per cent favor general trade.

	Communist China should be admitted to U.N.	Good idea to sell food products	Favor allowing business trade
All adults	37%	44%	40%
Minneapolis, St. Paul, and Duluth combined	42	46	45
Smaller cities	38	39	37
Rural nonfarm	29	44	39
Rural farm	39	56	46
Adults with grade school training	23	43	36
High school	38	45	39
College	48	44	47

DISCUSSION

ROOSA: Did Canada have difficulty receiving payments from China for the wheat shipments? In what way was Canada paid—in pounds, dollars, gold, or Chinese export goods? How does China deal with the problem of maintaining a balance of trade with its partners?

HAMILTON: The first sale, which took place in December–January, 1960–61, was for cash in the form of documents on the Bank of England. Long-term agreements, which have been in effect since April, 1961, are based on 25 per cent cash (again on the Bank of England) and 75 per cent in the form of notes—in the first instance for six months. More recently, they have been 18-month notes. They have been paid right on time and, 90 per cent of the time, paid in advance. In this context, let me relate an anecdote.

In one of the discussions that we had on the first long-term agreement in March or April of 1961, the Chinese negotiators pointed out that, according to their reading of the doctrines of Karl Marx, interest was a capitalistic innovation. Therefore, there should not be any interest on these short-term loans of six months. My answer was that I knew that Marx had had a very poor opinion of this matter of interest, but a fundamental principle of Marx was that no good socialist should ever take advantage of workers. I pointed out the sections of Marx's writings to them and indicated that this wheat did not belong to me but to our workers, the farmers. I depicted them getting up at the crack of dawn and going to bed at 10 o'clock at night and emphasized that I did not want to exploit them by having them turn their wheat over to the Chinese and then have to borrow money to live on from the banks, for which they would have to pay 5 per cent interest. If the Chinese did not pay that 5 per cent, it would be exploitation of the workers for whom I was working.

Then we adjourned. Two days later, they came back and said that I had made a good point. "We will pay 5 per cent and an additional one-half per cent," they said, "to make absolutely sure that no one says we are exploiting your workers."

ROOSA: There is in many instances an effort on the part of the Chinese negotiators to get an even balance in trade. That is not always possible, and they have to try to pick up a little in earnings on one front to meet the deficit in payments on another. China's exports to Hong Kong last year, if anything I have ever seen has even rough significance, were something on the order of a half-billion dollars. The imports were much smaller. Exports to Hong Kong are one of the means by which China is able to acquire foreign exchange to meet, for example, the fairly large continuing deficit that it has had in trade with Japan and also with West Germany. Someone has already mentioned that the West Germans, who have no diplomatic relations with China, have now reached second place behind Japan in exports to China. They are about to try to find ways of importing more, because the Chinese themselves apply this bilateral barter pressure to try to bring up both sides of the balance sheet at the same time.

ECKSTEIN: China maintained a trade deficit up to 1954. That is, up to 1954 China annually imported more than it exported. Then, from 1955 until 1966, a period of eleven years, China maintained an annual export surplus. This was largely possible because the trade deficit was financed by Soviet loans in the early years. Soviet loans effectively ceased in 1955, whereupon the Chinese had to repay them. In order to do so, the Chinese had to maintain an export surplus. For the last two years, China has again had a trade deficit, which it has financed by drawing on invisibles.

Essentially, China has consistently maintained large trade surpluses with Hong Kong and Southeast Asia. In these two areas, China earns large amounts of sterling to pay promptly for the wheat imports from Australia and Canada. Another important point is that the Chinese import wheat, but they export rice. The energy content of rice is almost the same in terms of food calories as that of wheat, but rice earns a higher price than wheat. So the Chinese play a smart foreign-exchange game by exporting rice and importing wheat.

ROOSA: As we look at these questions, relevant magnitudes have to be kept in mind. It is still true that the total trade turnover of mainland China is roughly identical in size to the total trade turnover of the island of Taiwan. There is no question at all, though, that the gross potential of the mainland is great. Also, questions have been raised about how China is able to grant some foreign aid. Its aid carries the highest potential advertising component of any aid program I have ever heard of or seen. In the last year, as far as anyone can estimate it, a total equivalent of perhaps $50 million in Chinese aid has been disbursed. But the skill shown in selecting conspicuous projects and in giving them widespread publicity conveys an impression of much greater significance than we seem to achieve with any of our own aid programs.

QUESTION: [1] Given the approach of the Chinese to economic

---

[1] Originating from the audience.

organization, where, in relative terms, do you think the gross national product might be at the end of this decade or in ten or twenty years, assuming no wars or other interruptions?

GALENSON: The difficulty is that we simply do not know what type of basic development model the Chinese will choose to follow. They have a number of options. They can go back to the first five-year-plan approach, which was essentially the model pioneered by Stalin, a model that very quickly brought Russia up to the rank of a world power with a heavy industrial base, but at a terrible cost to the Russian people. Essentially, an entire generation of people was sacrificed to gain this objective.

On the other hand, the Chinese might move toward a more diversified model, such as that which seems to motivate the Indians at the present time, not concentrating to the same degree on heavy industry but paying more attention to the needs of consumers and particularly to the agricultural sector.

We have virtually no information on what is in the minds of the Chinese planners at the present time. There were some reports that there was to be a new five-year plan announced in 1968, but it never materialized. A second five-year plan, which was supposed to follow the first one in 1958, just evaporated in the midst of the Great Leap Forward. We simply do not know whether China has had a third five-year plan or whether it is operating under a five-year plan or even a one-year plan. As a result, no meaningful estimates can be made of what the national product of China will be in ten or twenty years.

One can make some estimates about the future size of the Chinese population. But unless there is a more rational approach to the economic problems of growth than the Chinese have shown up to now, they are going to have great difficulty in raising per capita national income because of the huge population pressure in an already overpopulated country.

HAMILTON: The Chinese themselves have no substantial statistics. As a result of talking to their top men at the ministerial and deputy ministerial levels, I have the feeling that they would like to know, too. I visited farms and factories and asked to see their records and found that they kept them in children's exercise books. That system does not lend itself to the complete decimal-point analysis that the quantitative economist uses in our countries. I think they are not just trying to keep information from the public—they simply do not have the statistics themselves.

Secondly, I cannot help reacting every time I hear about China's overpopulation. If you want to see overpopulation, take a look at a city like New York, at the United Kingdom, or northern France, but don't say that China is overpopulated. China has more agricultural potential than any country that I know of in the world. Once they have the big machines and the chemical fertilizers to enable them to grow two crops a year instead of one in the north and three instead of two in the south, their vast area can support a population of 2 to 3 billion without even straining their land.

The Chinese have the most effective birth control program I have witnessed—and I have witnessed the brutal abortion techniques in Japan, too. In China, every family remembers that they are only twenty years away from a famine year, and there are certain social pressures that the Chinese apply. A boy is not supposed to hold the hand of a girl until he is twenty-five years old and she is twenty-two. Then, when a couple does get married, they are provided with only two rooms. Those two rooms give the couple the message loudly and clearly. Secondly, upon marriage, couples are given one ration card for the husband and one for the wife and two more for any potential increase. This is a pretty good indicator of how limiting the size of the family is encouraged.

In every town and village that I visited, there are small shops that have all manner of gadgets to increase virility and, beside them, all the things that keep one from having to bear the penalty of that virility. Moreover, in traveling in China's ten big cities and in visiting farms in Szechwan and the western parts of Shansi, I have not seen big families. Their biggest population pressure is due to the fact that their social and health programs are lengthening people's lives.

ROOSA: It is a fact that, although China's arable land is about one-third the size of ours, it supports a population four times as large. Their total agricultural output, even in the basic commodities, is so large that the marginal amount imported is almost trivial. One reason why China imports is that imported products can be shipped to many of the urban centers on the coast or on major rivers, whereas there is only a limited interior road and rail network for the transportation of domestic produce from the farms to the cities.

QUESTION: Professor Galenson mentioned that in 1953 there was an increase in China's industrial output because the Chinese received a large amount of Soviet technical assistance. How did the Chinese pay for this increased aid? Was the increased industrial product also a reflection of the bumper crop of 1952?

GALENSON: The agricultural advance contributed the means of paying the Russians. The Russians were paid in food, clothing, and textiles for all the equipment they provided, including a number of large and complete plants they built in China. It is also true that the increase in industrial production would have been impossible without agriculture, but the critical nature of Russian support should not be underestimated. At that time, China could not have gotten the latest, most modern equipment delivered from any country in the world other than the Soviet Union.

IV.
On America's China Policy: Two Senators Speak

JACOB K. JAVITS

The giant of Asia in the 1970's and 1980's—in terms of its power potential as a modern state—will be Japan and not China; and, this basic reality, so persuasively explained by Professor Reischauer, is the proper starting point for a rethinking of U.S. China policy in the years ahead. It permits us to shed many of the fears and shibboleths that have distorted U.S. policy in Asia since 1945.

Among these are the questions of membership in the United Nations and diplomatic recognition. Neither of these issues needs to dominate U.S. policy thinking about Communist China. Peking is not actively seeking U.N. admission and has placed what seem to be deliberately unacceptable conditions on its participation in the United Nations.

It is my belief that, if we revise our policy along the lines I am going to suggest, a thaw may take place in U.S.-China relations over the next five years, making both admission to the United Nations and diplomatic recognition easy and natural—following a period of psychological readjustment on both sides. The point to be stressed is that our minds should not be set against it. Much the same point needs to be made with respect to Communist China, as we get the strong feeling that its leadership right now values highly—for domestic reasons of its own—a policy of enmity toward the United States.

The Nixon Administration has a great opportunity to bury the lingering pall of McCarthyism that continues subtly to inhibit thought and debate in this country concerning China. The United States paid a very heavy price during the McCarthy period in the destruction of many of our most perceptive China experts. It was not only a period of grave human injustice to individuals but also a period of grave damage to our national stock of intellectual resources and experience, which has seriously affected the clarity and accuracy of our perception of events in Asia.

Active measures should now be taken to banish the lingering inhibitions of McCarthyism within the State Department and other councils of government. The fact that the policy-making process continues to be affected by thought-taboos with respect to China is illustrated, in my judgment, by the nervous timidity with which the State Department has floated a few cautious trial balloons in recent years. The liberalization of travel regulations, for instance, did not evoke the wrath in congressional and editorial circles that some of our higher officials feared. On the contrary, Congress and the nation at large welcomed the changes, frequently with expressions of mild surprise that they were so belated and so timid. The people are well ahead of the government on this matter!

The Nixon Administration has a unique opportunity to encourage and stimulate creative, new, and unorthodox thoughts about China, not only within the government but also in the nation as a whole. The overriding mandate given to President Nixon in the last election was to end the Vietnam War. The complicated drama of our national disengagement from that miscalculated war could well be used as an instrument for public education with respect to realities about China and Asia in general.

There are several lessons to be learned from the Vietnam War with respect to China. The first is that, for all its verbal violence, China has demonstrated unmistakable military prudence throughout that conflict. This prudence—China's deliberate abstention from any military involvement—has exposed to serious question much of the official rationale of the Johnson Administration for the Vietnam War. The argument that our involvement in Vietnam is a necessary stand against Chinese Communist expansionism is inconsistent with the actual record of Chinese behavior with respect to Vietnam.

Available evidence also indicates that China is likely to continue to exercise prudence with respect to the nuclear weapons capability it is acquiring at such great cost. At one heated point during the Vietnam debate, Secretary Rusk conjured a frightening image of "a billion Chinese on the mainland, armed with nuclear weapons." But not long afterward, former Assistant Secretary of Defense Warnke summarized the Pentagon's official assessment of Chinese policy in the following terms:

> We see no reason to conclude that the Chinese are any less cautious than the rulers of other nations that have nuclear weapons . . . Indeed, the Chinese have shown a disposition to act cautiously and to avoid any military clash with the United States that could lead to nuclear war.

In addition, the sharply rising tension along China's northern border with the Soviet Union—which has produced a number of military clashes in recent days—may induce Peking to seek a relaxation of tension in Southeast Asia and thereby facilitate a Vietnam settlement. It is also conceivable that the new focus being placed in Communist China on the territories "lost" to the Soviet Union through the so-called unequal treaties of the nineteenth century may, at some point, lessen Peking's obsession over the "recovery" of Taiwan.

I do not wish to suggest that we are about to witness an end to China's truculence. Rather, my point is that if we focus our attention on China's actions rather than its verbiage and upon its actual military capabilities, as opposed to its revolutionary aspirations, we must conclude that China does not necessarily present a significant military threat to our security.

It is really not surprising that China should project an image to the world of being a desperate and hysterical nation. No nation has ever faced such a formidable combination of problems. The challenge of organizing 800 million people into a single political and economic unit is awesome in itself. The simultaneous effort to modernize and radicalize such a mass of humanity complicates the problems of leadership immensely. The collision in this the oldest of human societies between the force of tradition and the force of revolution will continue to reverberate throughout the world for years to come.

China is struggling to become an industrial society, while the United States, Japan, and perhaps the Soviet Union are preparing their transition into a new order—the post-industrial nations of computers and nuclear and space technology—which is a quantum leap beyond the stage China is now so painfully and laboriously seeking to attain.

The immediate task for the United States is to formulate a policy that will facilitate China's peaceful integration into the broader Asia scene. In this regard, I believe that it would be to our interest to encourage, rather than discourage, trade and other contacts between Communist China and its non-Communist Asian neighbors. Similarly, and of course strictly for nonstrategic goods, we should encourage, rather than discourage, our European allies to trade with Peking.

There is a danger that the smaller nations of South and Southeast Asia could be overawed by China in one-to-one encounters. But there is now widespread recognition of that danger, as evidenced by the impressive trend toward cooperative regional organizations in non-Communist Asia. The United States should certainly support and encourage regional organization and economic and social integration in Asia, while we resist the temptation to try to lead it.

If a relaxation of our own zealous ideological opposition to China leads to a similar lessening of the anti-Communist ardor of some of our close allies in Asia—such as the Philippines and Thailand—we must take this calmly. For the lesson of the past twenty years has been that nationalism, and nationalism alone, is an effective barrier against the extension of Chinese-style Communism in Asia. This requires a shift of emphasis in our education and information efforts in Asia. The virtues of viable and progressive national integrity, rather than the dangers and evils of Chinese Communism, should be the focus of our efforts.

A more sophisticated and discriminating perception of the Asia scene on our part will alert us to numerous strains and tensions within parts of non-Communist Asia. A recognition of these tensions—some of which are of great antiquity—can save us from the reflex response that in the past has tended to make us view all trouble in Asia as being caused by Peking.

However, the fact is that ethnic tensions and rivalry between Malays and Chinese—which play such a crucial role in the policies of Indonesia, Malaysia, and the Philippines—are historic phenomena whose roots long predate the emergence of a Communist regime in Peking. The defeat of the September 30–October 1, 1965, coup attempted by the Chinese-dominated Communist party in Indonesia was due more to ethnic differences than to any ideological factors as understood in the West.

It would be well for our policy-makers to bear in mind that historic differences among the Thais, the Cambodians, and the Vietnamese will persist beyond the Vietnam War.

Another, most poignant, human drama is being enacted throughout the Himalayan foothills stretching from eastern India to the central highlands of Vietnam. Throughout that broad expanse, ancient aboriginal tribes, which sought haven in the mountains many years ago, are being pressed relentlessly by the dominant lowlanders, who are acquiring the means to extend their political, cultural, and economic writ into areas never really governed before by central authority. In some respects, this process resembles a slow-motion re-enactment of the destruction of the American Indian in this country in the nineteenth century.

In desperation, some of these doomed peoples will seek Chinese arms and Chinese support, as the Naga tribesmen of India and Burma have now begun to do. When this occurs, the United States must refrain from viewing the resultant clashes with central authorities as holy battles against Chinese Communist expansionism but recognize them for what they are—the birth pains of the development of nations.

Asia will be the scene of turmoil and commotion for many years to come. China, as the heart of eastern Asia in demographic and geographic terms, will be a leading participant in this tumult. Much of the turbulence we can expect will be of no legitimate security concern to the United States, and most of it will be beyond our power to control in any event.

But, in addition to the clamor and the conflict, there will be many creative and positive developments throughout Asia in which we can play a legitimate and rewarding major role. There is no need to fear that moving away from the role of an activist military involvement in Asia will lead to a U.S. withdrawal from Asia or to an abdication from our inescapable role as a major Pacific power. We can be sure that the nations of Asia will make demands upon our attention, our energies, and our resources beyond our capacity to fulfill. We will not need to go looking for work in Asia. But we must see to it that our efforts there are concentrated on productive and worthwhile enterprises and are not frittered away on mistaken military or ideological adventures.

In closing, I repeat what I said at the beginning: I do not foresee the possibility of a dramatic improvement in U.S.-China bilateral relations in the near future. Rather, we must anticipate—and use creatively—a period of mutual psychological readjustment. There is no justification for the United States to adopt a posture of *mea culpa* with respect to China, as some have advocated. Moreover, even if it were justified, I do not think such a posture would evoke a positive response from Peking. In my judgment, China will be much more impressed with, and responsive to, a policy of prudence and restraint that is also a policy of conviction and dignity.

China today probably has the rawest nerves and touchiest sensibilities of any nation in the world. We should recognize the historical reasons for this, but we cannot accommodate many of these neuroses. They can be worked out only internally, within China's national consciousness. For instance, no nation likes political partition—not the Chinese, nor the Germans, nor the Koreans, nor the Irish. But there are times when the international situation is such that a nation has to live with partition for a time. The maintenance of a separate political status for Taiwan doubtlessly is galling to Peking. But the fact that the peoples involved are Chinese does not raise the issue to a higher, almost apocalyptic level in the eyes of the other four-fifths of humanity. Peking's compulsive insistence that nothing can be discussed until Taiwan is first "returned" is a manifestation of Chinese racial arrogance, which we ought not to placate for its own sake. In my judgment, the future of Taiwan can be settled only by the will of the people of Taiwan themselves.

It is to be hoped that, as the United States adjusts its

perceptions, attitudes, and policies with respect to China, China will also begin to adjust its perceptions, attitudes, and policies toward the United States. Perhaps this process could be expedited by gestures or actions on our part that neither require nor expect a response from China. We have already heard suggestions about reciprocal educational and scientific exchange, especially in medicine and agriculture, about exchanging journalists, tourism, and humanitarian food sales.

I suggest that we consider whether it might be possible to make available on a private, nonreciprocal basis some of the fruits of our technology that might be of peaceful and humanitarian help to the Chinese people. For instance, the revolutionary type of ecological, geological, and meteorological photography that has resulted from the *Apollo* space program could be furnished to the Chinese authorities through nonofficial scientific channels. The result might be improved agricultural or flood-control programs, which would ease the lot of the hard-pressed Chinese peasantry.

EDWARD M. KENNEDY

This conference is one of the most important public sessions on China policy in recent years. That fact alone is extremely significant. The time at which this conference is being held is also significant. For, if we ever hoped that the Communist regime in China would disappear, our hope is in ruins today, as two powerful nations—China and the Soviet Union—engage in a continuing struggle for domination of the world Communist movement.

Thousands of American soldiers are dying in Vietnam in a land war in Asia whose purpose, we are told, is the containment of Peking. Demonstrations against American bases in Japan and Okinawa—bases built in part to contain China— shake the foundation of Japan. The shadow of Peking hangs dark over the discussions in Paris and over virtually every conference we attend on arms control. The success of the Nuclear Nonproliferation Treaty, on which the ink is hardly dry, depends in large part on the participation of China.

If we ever hoped that somehow our relations with China

could be stabilized at a point of rigid hostility without domestic sacrifice, our hope was dashed when we were told this spring by our government that we must now spend $7 billion as a down payment to protect our missiles and our nation from nuclear attack by China.

It is for these reasons that I consider this conference and what can come from it so important to the foreign policy of our nation. It is imperative that the issues you have discussed for so long become part of the national agenda of the United States. For almost twenty years, the United States has pursued the same unyielding policy of military containment and diplomatic isolation toward Communist China. However valid that policy may have seemed for the cold war of the 1950's, it is demonstrably false in the 1960's, and must not be carried into the 1970's.

Every new administration has a new opportunity to rectify the errors of the past. Each such opportunity consists in large part of the precious gift of time—time in which the good intentions of the government are presumed, time in which the normal conflicts of politics are suspended, time in which the new government has a chance to show that it is not tied to the policies of its predecessor.

If the Nixon Administration allows this time to pass without new initiatives, if it allows inherited policies to rush unimpeded along their course, it will have wasted this opportunity; it will have compromised the promises it made to the American people; and, worst of all, it will have disappointed the hopes and expectations of the world.

This is especially true in Vietnam. There is growing impatience with the continuing loss of American lives and the seeming frustration of our hopes for the reduction of violence and for the reduction of the American commitment. The advent of a new administration affords a moment of hope for millions of Americans and Vietnamese. It is a moment that will not long be with us.

The same opportunity exists for our policies throughout Asia. That is why it is all the more important that you who have been involved in the formulation and evaluation of those policies, both in private life and public service, meet here at this time to chart your recommendations.

For twenty years, our China policy has been a war policy. For far too long, we have carried out hostile measures of political, diplomatic, and economic antagonism toward one of the world's most important nations.

Now we must turn away from our policy of war and pursue a policy of peace. We must seek a new policy, not because of any supposed weakness in our present position or because we are soft on China, but because it is in our own national interest and the interest of all nations. By its sheer size and population, China deserves a major place in the world. As a nuclear power and a nation of 750 million citizens— likely to exceed 1 billion by the 1980's—China demands a voice in world efforts to deal with arms control and population control, with Asian security and international economic development, with all the great issues of our time.

Yet sixteen years after the end of the Korean War, we do not trade with China. We have no scientific or cultural exchanges. We oppose the representation of China in the United Nations. We refuse to give any sort of diplomatic recognition to the Communist regime on the mainland and continue to recognize the Nationalist regime of Chiang Kai- shek on Taiwan as the government of all China. Instead of developing ways to coexist with China in peace, we assume China will attack us as soon as it can, and we prepare to spend billions to meet that threat.

By some cruel paradox, an entire generation of young Americans and young Chinese have grown to maturity with their countries in a state of suspended war toward one another. Tragically, the world's oldest civilization and the world's most modern civilization, the world's most populous nation and the world's richest and most powerful nation, glare at each other across the abyss of nuclear war.

The division between us goes back to American support of the Chinese Nationalist regime during World War II and to the immediate postwar struggle between the Communists and the Nationalists. In the beginning, our policy was uncertain. The Communists gained power over the mainland in 1949. Between then and the outbreak of the Korean War in 1950, the United States seemed to be preparing to accept the fact of the Chinese revolution. After the retreat of the Nationalists to Taiwan, our government refused to go to their aid and refused to place the American Seventh Fleet in the Taiwan Strait to prevent a Communist takeover of the island. To do so, we said, would be to intervene in the domestic civil war between the Communists and the Nationalists.

This policy was fully debated by the Congress and the public. Although we deplored the Communist rise to power, we recognized that we could do nothing to change it. We anticipated that we would soon adjust to the new Asian reality by establishing relations with the Communist regime.

This situation changed overnight on June 25, 1950, when North Korea attacked South Korea. Fearing that the attack foreshadowed a Communist offensive throughout Asia, the United States ordered the Seventh Fleet into the Taiwan Strait and sent large amounts of military aid to the weak Nationalist government on the island. To the Communists, the meaning was clear. We would use force to deny Taiwan to the new mainland government, even though both the Communists and the Nationalists agreed that the island was Chinese.

Shortly thereafter, in response to the attempt of our forces to bring down the North Korean Government by driving toward the Chinese border, China entered the Korean War. With hindsight, most experts agree that China's action in Korea was an essentially defensive response, launched to prevent the establishment of a hostile government on its border. At the time, however, the issue was far less clear. At the request of the United States, the United Nations formally branded China as an aggressor, a stigma that rankles Peking's leaders even today.

While we fought the Chinese in Korea, we carried out a series of political and economic actions against their country. We imposed a total embargo on all American trade with the mainland. We froze Peking's assets in the United States. We demanded that our allies limit their trade with China. We conducted espionage and sabotage operations against the mainland and supported similar efforts by the Nationalists. We began to construct a chain of bases, encircling China with American military power, including nuclear weapons.

It is not my purpose here to question the merits of the actions we took while fighting China in Korea. We all remember the climate of those times and the great concern of our country with Chinese military actions. Today, however, sixteen years after the Korean armistice was signed, we have taken almost no significant steps to abandon our posture of war toward China and to develop relations of peace.

Let us look at our policy from the viewpoint of Peking: China's leaders see the United States supporting the Nationalists' pretense to be the government of the mainland. They see thousands of American military personnel on Taiwan. American warships guard the waters between the mainland and Taiwan. American nuclear bases and submarines ring the periphery of China. The United States supports Nationalist U-2 flights over the mainland, as well as Nationalist guerrilla raids and espionage. Hundreds of thousands of American soldiers are fighting in Vietnam to contain China. America applies constant diplomatic and political pressure to deny Peking a seat in the United Nations, to deny it diplomatic recognition by the nations of the world, and to deny it freedom of trade. We turn our nuclear warheads toward China.

And now we prepare to build a vast ABM system to protect ourselves against China. In light of all these facts, what Chinese leader would dare to propose anything but the deepest hostility toward the United States?

With respect to the ABM question, I am strongly opposed for many reasons to the deployment of the Pentagon's system. For the purpose of the present discussion, however, one of its most significant drawbacks is that it is likely to be seen in Peking as a new military provocation by the United States. Our overwhelming nuclear arsenal already provides adequate deterrence against any temptation by Peking to engage in a first strike against the United States. From the Chinese perspective, the only utility of an American ABM system is to defend the United States against whatever feeble response Peking could muster after an American first strike against China. Far from deterring aggression by China, therefore, deployment of the ABM system will simply add fuel to our warlike posture toward China. It will increase Chinese fears of American attack and will encourage China's leaders to embark on new steps in the development of their nuclear capability. Apart from the technical and other policy objections that exist against the ABM system, I believe it makes no sense from the standpoint of a rational Asia policy for America.

In large part, our continuing hostility toward China after the Korean War has rested on a hope that is now obviously forlorn, a hope that, under a policy of military containment and political isolation, the Communist regime on the mainland would be a passing phenomenon and would eventually be repudiated by the Chinese people. Few of us today have any serious doubt that Communism is permanent for the fore-seeable future on the mainland. There is no believable prospect that Chiang Kai-shek and the Nationalists will return to power there, however regrettable we may regard that fact.

Surely, in the entire history of American foreign policy, there has been no fiction more palpably absurd than our official position that Communist China does not exist. For twenty years, the Nationalists have controlled only the 2 million Chinese and the 11 million Taiwanese on the island of Taiwan, 100 miles from the mainland of China. How long will we continue to insist that the rulers of Taiwan are also the rulers of the hundreds of millions of Chinese on the millions of square miles of the mainland? It is as though the island of Cuba were to claim sovereignty over the entire continent of North America.

The folly of our present policy of isolating China is matched by its futility. Almost all other nations have adjusted to the reality of China. For years, Peking has had extensive diplomatic, commercial, and cultural relations with a number of the nations in the world, including many of our closest allies. Outside the United Nations, our policy of quarantine toward China has failed. To the extent that the Communist regime is isolated at all, it is isolated largely at China's own choosing, and not as a consequence of any effective American policy.

Our actions toward China have rested on the premise that the People's Republic is an illegitimate, evil, and expansionist regime that must be contained until it collapses or at least begins to behave in conformity with American interests. Secretary of State Dulles was the foremost exponent of this moralistic view, carrying it to the extent that he even refused to shake hands with Chou En-lai at the Geneva Conference in 1954. That slight has not been forgotten.

The Communist regime was said to be illegitimate because, we claimed, it had been imposed on the supposedly unreceptive Chinese people by agents of the Soviet Union. Communist China, according to this view, was a mere Soviet satellite. One Assistant Secretary in the State Department called it a Soviet Manchukuo, suggesting that China's new leaders were no more independent than were the Chinese puppets whom Japan installed in Manchuria in the 1930's. This evaluation grossly exaggerated the extent to which Soviet aid was responsible for the Communist takeover of China, and the events of the past decade—amply confirmed by the intense hostility of the recent border clashes—have shattered the myth of Soviet domination of China.

The Communist regime was said to be evil because of the great violence and deprivation of freedom that it inflicted on millions of people who opposed its rise to power. Obviously, we cannot condone the appalling cost in human life and suffering of the Chinese revolution. Yet, in many other cases, we have recognized revolutionary regimes, especially when the period of revolutionary excess has passed. Even in the case of the Soviet Union, the United States waited only sixteen years to normalize relations with the revolutionary government.

Unfortunately, we have tended to focus exclusively on the costs of the Chinese revolution. We have ignored the historical conditions that evoked it and the social and economic gains it produced. We have ignored the fact that the Nationalists also engaged in repressive measures and deprivations of freedom, not only during their tenure on the mainland, but also on Taiwan. We have created a false image of a struggle between "Free China" and "Red China," between good and evil. Given our current perspective and the greater understanding of revolutionary change that has come with time, we can now afford a more dispassionate and accurate review of the Chinese revolution.

Finally, there is the charge that the Communist regime is an expansionist power. At bottom, it is this view that has given rise to our containment policy in Asia, with the enormous sacrifices it has entailed. The charge that the Communist regime is expansionist has meant different things at different times. On occasion, American spokesmen have conjured up the image of a "Golden Horde" or "Yellow Peril" that would swoop down over Asia. Today, most leaders in Washington employ more responsible rhetoric, and it is the Russians who perpetuate this image of China.

Virtually no experts on China expect Peking to commit aggression, in the conventional sense of forcibly occupying the territory of another country—as the Soviet Union recently occupied Czechoslovakia. Such action is in accord neither with past Chinese actions nor with present Chinese capabilities. Despite their ideological bombast, the Chinese Communists have in fact been extremely cautious about risking military involvement since the Korean War. The Quemoy crises of the 1950's and the 1962 clash with India were carefully limited engagements. The struggle over Tibet is widely regarded as a reassertion of traditional Chinese jurisdiction over that remote area. China has not used force to protect the overseas Chinese in the disturbances in Burma, Malaysia, or Indonesia. Its navy and air force are small. It can neither transport its troops nor supply them across the long distances and difficult terrain of a prolonged war of aggression.

Obviously, our concern today is not so much the danger of direct Chinese aggression as the danger of indirect aggression, based on Chinese efforts to subvert existing governments and replace them with governments friendly to Peking. Yet, until Vietnam led to our massive involvement in Southeast Asia, Peking enjoyed only very limited success in its attempts to foster "wars of national liberation." Although China, of course, will claim to play a role wherever political instability occurs in Asia, Africa, and even Latin America, its record of subversion is unimpressive. On the basis of the past, it is very likely that nations whose governments work for equality and social justice for their people will be able to overcome any threat of Chinese subversion.

Furthermore, we can expect that time will moderate China's revolutionary zeal. Experience with the Soviet Union and the Eastern European Communist nations suggests that the more fully China is brought into the world community, the greater will be the pressure to behave like a nation-state, rather than a revolutionary power.

Ironically, it is Communist China's former teacher, the Soviet Union, that is now determined to prevent any moderation of Chinese-American hostility. We cannot accept at face value the current Soviet image of China, for the Soviets have far different interests in Asia than we do. Although we must persist in our efforts to achieve wider agreement with Moscow, we must not allow the Russians to make continuing hostility toward Peking the price of future Soviet-American cooperation. Rather than retard our relations with Moscow, a Washington-Peking thaw might well provide the Soviet Union with a badly needed incentive to improve relations with us.

We must not, however, regard relations with Peking and Moscow as an "either/or" proposition. We must strive to improve relations with both. We must be alert, therefore, to any opportunity offered by the escalating hostility between China and the Soviet Union to ease our own tensions with those nations.

Both of us—Chinese and Americans alike—are prisoners of the passions of the past. What we need now, and in the decades ahead, is liberation from those passions. Given the history of our past relations with China, it is unrealistic to expect Peking to take the initiative. It is our obligation. We are the great and powerful nation, and we should not condition our approach on any favorable action or change of attitude by Peking. For us to begin a policy of peace would be a credit to our history and our place in the world today. To continue on our present path will lead only to further hostility and the real possibility of mutual destruction.

Of course, we must not delude ourselves. Even if the United States moves toward an enlightened China policy, the foreseeable prospects for moderating Chinese-American tensions are not bright. It is said that there is no basis for hope so long as the current generation of Communist Chinese leaders remains in power. This may well be true. Yet, Peking's invitation last November to resume the Warsaw talks, although later withdrawn, suggests the possibility that China's policy may change more rapidly than outside observers can now anticipate.

We must remember, too, that the regime in Peking is not a monolith. As the upheavals of the Great Leap Forward and the Cultural Revolution have shown, China's leaders are divided by conflicting views and pressures for change. We must seek to influence such change in a favorable direction. We can do so by ensuring that reasonable options for improved relations with the United States are always available to Peking's moderate or less extreme leaders.

The steps that we take should be taken soon. Even now, the deterioration of Sino-Soviet relations in the wake of the recent border clashes may be stimulating at least some of the leaders in Peking to re-evaluate their posture toward the United States and provide us with an extraordinary opportunity to break the bonds of distrust.

What can we do to hasten the next opportunity? Many of us here tonight are already on record as favoring a more positive stand. We must actively encourage China to adopt the change in attitude for which we now simply wait. We must act now to make clear to the Chinese and to the world that the responsibility for the present impasse no longer lies with us.

First, and most important, we should proclaim our willingness to adopt a new policy toward China—a policy of peace, not war, a policy that abandons the old slogans, embraces today's reality, and encourages tomorrow's possibility. We should make clear that we regard China as a legitimate power in control of the mainland, entitled to full participation as an equal member of the world community and to a decent regard for its own security. The policy I advocate will in no way impede our ability to respond firmly and effectively to any possibility of attack by the Chinese. What it will do, however, is emphasize to China that our military posture is purely defensive and that we stand ready at all times to work toward improvement in our relations.

Second, we should attempt to reconvene the Warsaw talks. At the time the talks were canceled, I wrote the Secretary of State, asking the Administration to make an urgent new attempt to establish the contact that we so nearly achieved at Warsaw and to do so before the air of expectancy that hung over the talks was completely dissipated. If the talks are resumed, we should attempt to transform them into a more confidential and perhaps more significant dialogue. The parties might meet on an alternating basis in their respective embassies, or even in their respective countries, rather than in a palace of the Polish Government. Whether or not the talks are resumed, more informal official and semi-official conversations with China's leaders should be offered.

Third, we should unilaterally do away with restrictions on travel and nonstrategic trade. We should do all we can to promote exchanges of people and ideas, through scientific and cultural programs and access by news media representatives. In trade, we should place China on the same footing as the Soviet Union and the Communist nations of Eastern Europe. We should offer to send trade delegations and even a resident trade mission to China and to receive Chinese trade delegations and a Chinese trade mission in this country. Finally, we should welcome closer contacts between China and the rest of the world, rather than continue to exert pressure on our friends to isolate the Peking regime.

Fourth, we should announce our willingness to re-establish the consular offices we maintained in the People's Republic during the earliest period of Communist rule, and we should welcome Chinese consular officials in the United States. Consular relations facilitate trade and other contacts. They frequently exist in the absence of diplomatic relations and often pave the way for the establishment of such relations.

Fifth, we should strive to involve the Chinese in serious arms control talks. We should actively encourage them to begin to participate in international conferences, and we should seek new opportunities to discuss Asian security and other problems.

Sixth, we should seek, at the earliest opportunity, to discuss with China's leaders the complex question of the establishment of full diplomatic relations. For the present, we should continue our diplomatic relations with the Nationalist regime on Taiwan and guarantee the people of that island against any forcible takeover by the mainland. To Peking at this time, the question of diplomatic recognition seems to be unavoidably linked to the question of whether we will withdraw recognition from the Nationalists and the question of whether Taiwan is part of the territory of China. Both the Communists and the Nationalists claim Taiwan as part of China, but our own government regards the status of the island as undefined, even though we maintain diplomatic relations with the Nationalists.

We have failed to agree on solutions involving other divided countries and peoples—as in Germany—and we cannot be confident of greater success in the matter of Taiwan. There are critical questions that simply cannot now be answered:

Will the minority regime of the Chinese Nationalists continue to control the island's Taiwanese population?

Will the Taiwanese majority eventually transform the island's government through the exercise of self-determination?

Will an accommodation be worked out between a future Taiwan Government and the Peking regime on the mainland?

To help elicit Peking's interest in negotiations, we should withdraw our token American military presence from Taiwan. This demilitarization of Taiwan could take place at no cost to our treaty commitments or to the security of the island. Yet it would help to make clear to Peking our desire for the Communists, the Nationalists, and the Taiwanese to reach a negotiated solution on the status of the island.

A dramatic step like unilateral recognition of Peking would probably be an empty gesture at this time. As the experience of France implies, unilateral recognition of Peking is not likely to be effective unless it is accompanied by the withdrawal of our existing recognition of the Nationalists. And, as the case of Great Britain suggests, Peking may insist on our recognition of the mainland's claim to Taiwan before allowing us to establish full ambassadorial relations. These problems will have to be negotiated, and we should move now to start the process.

Seventh, without waiting for resolution of the complex question of Taiwan, we should withdraw our opposition to Peking's entry into the United Nations as the representative of China, not only in the General Assembly, but also in the Security Council and other organs. The Security Council seat was granted to China in 1945 in recognition of a great people who had borne a major share of the burden in World War II, thereby making the United Nations possible. It was not a reward for the particular political group that happened to be running the country at the time.

In addition, we should work within the United Nations to attempt to assure representation for the people on Taiwan that will reflect the island's governmental status. It may be that the Chinese Nationalists can continue to enjoy a seat in the General Assembly. Or, if an independent republic of Taiwan emerges, it might be admitted into the United Nations as a new state. Possibly, if a political accommodation is reached between the Communist regime on the mainland and the government on Taiwan, the people of Taiwan might be represented in the United Nations as an autonomous unit of China, by analogy to the present status in the United

Nations of Byelorussia and the Ukraine as autonomous provinces of the Soviet Union.

From its inception, the United Nations has displayed remarkable flexibility in adjusting to political realities. There are many possible solutions to the China problem in the United Nations. Without insisting on any one, we should move now to free the United Nations to undertake the long-delayed process of adjusting to the reality of the People's Republic of China, and we should clearly indicate to Peking our willingness to discuss these questions.

In dealing with the problems of diplomatic recognition and United Nations representation, I have placed primary emphasis on the need to initiate discussions with Peking in these areas. Since it is impossible to predict when or how the Chinese will respond to a change in American policy, we cannot maintain a hard and fast position on these questions. We cannot afford to close any options by endorsing detailed schemes at this time. What we can do, however, is act now on the broad range of initiatives I have mentioned and make clear to Peking that our views are not rigid on even the most difficult issues that have divided us so bitterly in recent years.

We will have to be patient. Peking's initial reaction to serious initiatives on our part will probably be a blunt refusal. But, by laying the groundwork now for an improved relationship in the 1970's and beyond, we will be offering the present and future leaders in Peking a clear and attractive alternative to the existing impasse in our relations.

Perhaps I can sum up my central theme in terms that you may find appropriate. According to Chinese tradition, the model Confucian gentleman was taught that, whenever involved in a dispute, he should first examine his own behavior, ask himself whether he bears some responsibility for the dispute, and take the initiative to try to arrive at a harmonious settlement.

It may prove futile for us to follow this advice when dealing with Chinese who claim to reject many of China's great traditions. But we will never know unless we try. If nothing changes, we Americans will have to live with the consequences of arms and fear and war. We owe ourselves, we owe the future, a heavy obligation to try.

V.
Other Countries, Different Views

KENNETH T. YOUNG

For almost a century, the question of China has perplexed statesmen, scholars, and people everywhere. In the 1970's, the China question will be even more complex than ever and will certainly remain difficult for Americans to understand.

We tend to be two-dimensional about China. We look at the problem either on the basis of purely bilateral problems or else in terms of what other governments wish we would do about the People's Republic of China and the Republic of China. Our own discussion has tended toward the opposites of recognition and United Nations membership or exclusion and containment.

We not only need more information about mainland China; we must also develop multidimensional angles of vision. We need to see the complexities of the China question in today's fast-changing world; 1970 is not 1950. The Asian outlook has changed radically. We need to become more objective and better informed than we have been over the past generations. It will be the interaction of this complex world context with

China, rather than primarily American action, which may some day persuade Chinese leaders to join the world, the world as it is evolving, rather than the world that they would like to remake in their particular image.

The four commentaries of this chapter will help us do all these things. By listening to a Canadian diplomat, Ambassador Chester Ronning, a European sovietologist, Dr. Klaus Mehnert, an Indian diplomat, Ambassador Arthur Lall, and a British humanist, Lady Jackson (Barbara Ward), we can broaden our perspective on the whole range of the China question. We Americans are not so likely to think of these different angles of vision—Canadian, German, Indian, and British—which do not represent merely national views but which reflect several major aspects of the China question with which we should be directly concerned, whether we realize it or not. For example, we heed Ambassador Ronning's warning that China plays a vital role in the solution of Asian problems and that it is deeply concerned about the U.S. role in Asia. Many of Asia's problems, and China's, as he justly points out, are related to the global separation of rich nations from poor ones.

We often forget that the Chinese people have been coping with the "lopsided" impact, as Barbara Ward puts it, of Western intervention for more than a century. The evolution of China's relations with the Americans, the Russians, and, particularly, the Asians will perhaps be determined largely by the way in which China and the Asian countries cope with the modernization crisis. It broadens our outlook if we think of the China problem either in terms of a possible catastrophe in China caused by its failure to cope with modernization and the volcanic consequences such failure would have in Asia or, on the other hand, in terms of a possible success that the Chinese leadership and the Chinese people, *after Mao*, may find in dealing with mass modernization, which would have some meaning for the rest of the world. While the projections of these opposite contingencies are extremely difficult for any of us to make in the case of China, or the whole world, we should certainly be much more aware of what Barbara Ward calls the "global Molotov cocktail" about to explode in our midst.

I sometimes think that the development of Asia may well be the single most important key to China's future. I, therefore, welcome Ambassador Lall's emphasis on China's relations with the small countries and the big countries in Asia. This combination of the large and small Asian nations is indeed the basic international reality in Asia for us as well as for the Chinese people. I am not so sure, however, that the Chinese Communists have been or will remain so meticulous about their relations with the smaller countries of Asia, as Ambassador Lall indicates. Certainly, the Chinese People's Republic has caused difficulties in India, Burma, Thailand, Cambodia, Laos, and Indonesia. He is undoubtedly right, on the other hand, that China's relations with Japan, India and, I would add, Indonesia, will be difficult for a long time, because these are the large and competitive centers of actual and potential power with which the Chinese Communist leadership must contend if it remains belligerent, ambitious, and, in any way, expansionist. One can draw the inference from his remarks that workable relations among the smaller and larger countries in Asia—an Asian Concert—might go far to attract China's peaceful involvement, provided the Asians, as well as Europeans and Americans, do not irrationally generate even more paranoia in Peking than now exists.

These four speakers, directly or indirectly, refer to the basic issue of Sino-Soviet antagonism. The quarrel between China and the Soviet Union is not only very serious, as Dr. Mehnert points out, but it may be the most critical world problem of the next decade. If it degenerates into further hostilities, the whole world might end up ravaged. While we Americans must not harp on this morbid prospect, we should follow the suggestion of these speakers that the United States in particu-

lar, and the West in general, may have vital "mediatory in-
fluences," to use Ambassador Lall's well-taken phrase, in this
dangerous conflict. Certainly, we should do everything to
dampen the Russian "Boxer Rebellion" version of what is
going on in North Asia today.

This triangular relation—Washington, Peking, and Moscow
—is complex and dangerous because all three share much
suspicion and ignorance about each other. As I have written,
the United States may be the only one of the three that still
has a chance to keep its "cool," if for no other reason than to
counterbalance the rising emotions of the Chinese and the
Russians against each other. How we manage this triangular
relation will test the statesmanship of our officials and the
capacity of all of us as citizens.

Ambassador Ronning, Dr. Mehnert, Ambassador Lall, and
Lady Jackson (Barbara Ward) have contributed to deepening
our perceptions and extending our time frame for developing
a balanced perspective about all aspects of the China question.
In its broadest terms, this means searching for means to bring
about the association and articulation of all the Chinese people
with a peaceful but changing world structure.

CHESTER RONNING

Canadian public opinion, in general, supports the decision of our government to negotiate in Stockholm with representatives of the People's Republic of China mutually acceptable terms of recognition and of exchange of diplomatic missions.

Canada has given serious consideration to the problem of Canadian relations with China for the past twenty years, and it has finally decided to recognize the government of more than 700 million Chinese and to approve of their representation in the United Nations. Canada believes that it is important not merely to establish diplomatic relations with China but to use those relations as soon as possible to cooperate with China in efforts to promote peace in Asia. We support a change in the U.N. representation because we believe the objective of peace in Asia can only be obtained when all nations have become members of the United Nations.

Traditional American foreign policy in China was favored by Canadians in preference to the policies of the great European powers because American policy held greater promise to terminate foreign military interference in the internal affairs of China and to end foreign domination of China's own foreign policy. The United States, for example, proclaimed the "Open Door" policy, which purported to prevent the crystallization of the policy of dividing China into spheres of influence. The United States returned all its share of the Boxer indemnity to the Chinese for the education of Chinese students in the United States.[1]

The United States rejected any policy involving the use of the American army in interference in China's internal affairs. This was in contrast to the policy of other great powers, especially former tsarist Russia and former imperial Japan. These powers seldom hesitated to use any pretext whatever to annex Chinese territory. (The Soviet Union may still reap the whirlwind tsarist Russia started in such areas as Vladivostock.) When traditional American China policy is remembered, it is no wonder that Americans were greeted everywhere with *"mei-kuo jen ting hao"* ("Americans are very good").

The popularity of Americans in China, however, came to a sudden end after 1949, when the Communists won the civil war. Traditional American China policy was drastically changed. The Seventh Fleet was stationed in the Taiwan Strait to prevent the consummation of a complete victory in the civil war for the Chinese Communists. Taiwan was proclaimed to be strategic for the security of the United States in the Pacific. American military bases were established in a semi-circular chain around China from South Korea, Okinawa, and Taiwan to Vietnam and Thailand.

China was isolated by a military, trade, and economic blockade called containment and was considered to be a puppet of the Soviet Union, in spite of the fact that the

---

[1] The Boxer Rebellion at the end of the nineteenth century—primarily an antiforeign demonstration—resulted in foreign deaths and loss of property for which China later paid indemnities.

Chinese Communists had received almost no aid from Moscow during the civil war and had defied Russian advice consistently since 1927. The government in Peking was said to be forcing a foreign, Russian ideology down the throats of the Chinese people, an ideology they would never accept. The fact was that the new revolutionary ideology, which was intended to transform and modernize Chinese society and culture, was a pragmatic interpretation of Marxism-Leninism by Mao Tse-tung.

How completely American policy in Asia had changed became abundantly clear when the United States became gradually involved in the war in Vietnam and 500,000 American troops were deployed on the mainland of Asia. U.S. policy came around almost 180 degrees from traditional American military policy and began to resemble that of other great powers during the nineteenth century. The real enemy became "Asian Communism with its headquarters in Peking."

This seemed to be the situation only a little more than a decade after the 1954 comment made by General Bedell Smith in my hearing. When it was suggested that American troops be sent to relieve the French in Dien Bien Phu, he said, "No American boys are going to get bogged down in the jungles of Vietnam, except over my dead body."

Canada, disturbed by the acceleration of the bombing of North Vietnam, offered its good offices to both sides in an effort to find some common ground for direct contacts and dialogue leading to peaceful negotiations. It became evident to me during my visit to Hanoi for this purpose in 1966 that talks could not begin until there was an unconditional cessation of the bombing of North Vietnam. The welcome announcement by the President of the United States on October 31, 1968, that he had ordered the cessation of the bombing of all the territory of North Vietnam may become one of the most important decisions made by any President of the United States since World War II.

It would be wishful thinking indeed to conclude that this change of policy in Vietnam may indicate the possibility of a similar change in United States–China relations. It should not be beyond the realm of possibility, however, that the pressure the American people brought to bear on the President of the United States to force a reversal of policy in Vietnam could also begin to improve United States–China relations. At least, this is the impression I got from Senator Kennedy in his great speech. At any rate, my confidence was regained in the American people and in their capacity to prove that democratic processes in the United States are still operative.

United States–China relations have been so severely strained for such a long time that one wonders if there is any possibility of surmounting the mountainous obstacles that have seemingly become permanent. Nevertheless, President Nixon may have indicated where a beginning can be made eventually to jar loose the log jam of ill will, enmity, hatred, and suspicion. In commenting on the Chinese proposal of November, 1968, to discuss the principles of peaceful coexistence with the United States in Warsaw, he suggested that some trade in nonstrategic goods and an exchange of newspaper correspondents could become possible if the Chinese response was satisfactory. I suggest that the time is right for unilateral declarations by the United States regardless of response.

Canada's important wheat trade with China was a significant factor in paving the way for ultimate diplomatic relations. Would it be possible for the greatest power on earth to take the responsibility of announcing that the United States had decided unconditionally to remove restrictions on trade with China in nonstrategic goods and would welcome Chinese newspaper correspondents in the United States? It is not impossible that a beginning could thus be made for the contacts and dialogue that are so essential for peaceful negotiation of the issues that today seem impossible to resolve. If tensions could be lowered by means such as those proposed by Senator Kennedy so as to create an atmosphere in which intelligent discussion could take place, solutions might be found even for such problems as the future of Taiwan.

It is urgent that the West should understand what has really been happening in China in the Cultural Revolution, for example. It is important that the West should change the trend toward ignoring China even in the solution of Asian problems, such as that in Vietnam. As we move into the twenty-first century, the problems of the Far East can no longer be dealt with in terms of nineteenth-century concepts. Revolution has changed Asia.

We cannot escape the relationship of Asia's problems to the issue that more than any other divides our globe into two worlds and cuts across all other national and international issues—the separation of nations into two groups: the industrialized wealthy nations and the unindustrialized poor ones. This global problem can be dealt with only by a global approach.

Our best and perhaps only hope of ever solving that greatest of all international problems is through the United Nations. To make our only world organization effective, all nations must yield sufficient national sovereignty to create a permanent U.N. peace-keeping force. That body would enforce decisions by an international world court to which all international problems and disputes are submitted for peaceful settlement. A number of nations, including Canada, have signified their willingness to provide a permanent U.N. peace-keeping force.

It may be that a final solution of the United States–China relationship will not take place before all the great powers and potentially great powers, including China, cease trying to find security in the world power struggle and balance of power and start giving their support to the United Nations to make it a true world organization. In anticipation of that day and to create the atmosphere in which that ideal may become a reality, can the United States, leader of the Western powers, start by trading in nonstrategic goods with China and welcoming Chinese correspondents to the United States? My incurable optimism, raised to a higher level by Senator Kennedy's proposals, inclines me to believe that the United States will accept the responsibility and will take the initiative to establish better relations with China.

KLAUS MEHNERT

My analysis of the world environment and of China's role in it is built around seven theses.

First, as a result of World War II, the world became a bipolar one, and, in a sense, it still is. But a change is evident. The transition from a bipolar Soviet-American world to a multipolar one in which China is getting a say is an exciting development of this point in history, and it forces us to rethink the world situation.

The second thesis: Among the many question marks in Asia, there are two certainties—that there will be a time without Mao Tse-tung and a time without Chiang Kai-shek. The day is approaching when the two great antagonists of the last decades' struggle in China will no longer be on the political scene. What changes can be expected in China after their departure? As far as mainland China is concerned, there are two possibilities. One is that Maoism will live on after Mao; the other is that Maoism will die with him, perhaps not immediately but after some time, as Stalinism died in the Soviet

Union within three years of Stalin's death. To be sure, a certain resurrection of Stalinism is now under way in the Soviet Union; still, the change from Stalin to Khrushchev was momentous. Maoism is essentially a visionary utopianism rather than a practical political creed. If it disappears, its place will be taken by pragmatism, by those pragmatic people whom Mao calls the Khrushchevs of China.

With Chiang Kai-shek out of the picture, things will change in Taiwan also. It is very likely that the Taiwanese element—those people who did not come from the mainland in 1949 but who have lived for generations in Taiwan—will have more to say. Their attachment to mainland China is much less strong than that of the refugees of 1949 and of the people around Chiang Kai-shek.

My third thesis is that the American war in Vietnam is not a war against China, as many people for a long time were inclined to think. It is a war against the North Vietnamese, who fight largely with Soviet weapons. Thus, China could not stop the war in Vietnam, even if it wished to do so, while the Soviet Union could end it at any time by halting its shipments of military hardware.

Fourth, Hanoi and Ho Chi Minh [who has since died] are more independent of China today than was the case ten years ago. During recent years, the Vietnamese have shown tremendous stamina; as a result, Ho's stature as a Communist nationalist leader in Asia has risen everywhere and particularly among youth in Berkeley, Berlin, and all over the world. He has very cleverly played on the Sino-Soviet conflict and has established North Vietnam as a separate entity; it is certainly not a satellite of China. This nationalism of the Vietnamese (rather than their belief in Communism, which has not functioned very well in North Vietnam) is the primary explanation for their resistance. The nationalism of the Southeast Asian countries makes them less likely to be "dominoes" falling under Chinese domination than many, including myself, have previously assumed. The existence of popular nationalist leaders in Southeast Asian countries, such as Prince Sihanouk of Cambodia, is in the interest of the non-Communist world, even if they are not always easy to deal with.

Fifth, the Sino-Soviet quarrel is very serious indeed. Except for the profound antipathy between Arabs and Israelis, the Sino-Soviet dispute is the most bitter conflict in the world today. The depth of the hatred can be seen in what the Maoists and the Russians write about each other. To Mao, the Soviet Union is a daily reminder of what happens once the true belief is abandoned as the guiding light. Once the road of pragmatism is taken, the society, so Mao believes, becomes a bourgeois, bureaucratic, capitalist one, not very different from that of capitalist countries. Mao hates the Soviet Union particularly, because he feels that what is happening there can happen in China, too. Thus, in fighting the Khrushchevites in Russia, he is fighting the rise of their counterparts in China.

Today, there is practically no subject on which the Russians and Chinese agree. Not even the American bombing of North Vietnam could bring the Russians and the Chinese closer together, nor are they of one mind on the subject of revolutionary movements elsewhere. The Russians often attack such movements as anarchistic and adventuristic, while the Chinese praise them as Mao Tse-tung's thought in action.

The invasion of Czechoslovakia has created an additional fear in China, since the Russians, under the terms of the so-called Brezhnev doctrine, claim the right to enforce the proper creed upon other Communist countries and could move into China as they moved into Czechoslovakia. The bitterness of the fighting on the Ussuri River and the fact that the Chinese have played it up more than earlier incidents of this kind indicate that the Chinese want to show the Russians that they do not intend to be another Czechoslovakia.

Sixth, although the two great Communist powers, the

Soviet Union and China, have been shooting at each other throughout the 1960's—first with words and now with bullets—the Western world, which both the Russians and the Chinese say must be completely overthrown, has not made any political use of this conflict.

My seventh and last thesis: The fact that the Soviets and the Chinese are shooting at each other on the Ussuri River should not force us to take sides. The Soviet Union has tried very hard to stampede the Western world into an anti-Chinese, "Boxer Rebellion" attitude. It has sent its ambassadors to all the Western governments to charge that the Chinese have committed atrocities on the ice of the Ussuri. Let us not accept this simple, one-sided version of what is going on in the Far East today. Nor is there any reason to say that it is impossible to have good relations with both the Soviet Union and China.

As far as West Germany is concerned, there is only one reason why it does not establish formal relations with China as it has done with Rumania: Germany does not want to displease its most important ally, the United States. And for the United States, there really is no reason not to normalize relations with China, except for the fact that the Chinese, by calling off the meeting set for Warsaw on February 20, 1969, have shown that they are not inclined at the moment to go ahead in this direction. But that will change. The mood is changing in the United States too. There will be a willingness to talk on both sides in the not-too-distant future.

ARTHUR LALL

From the vantage point of Asia, China has three primary sets of relationships: with the small countries along its borders, with the larger Asian states, such as India and Japan, and with the two superpowers, the United States and the Soviet Union. I should like to make a prediction about the course of each of these relationships over the next ten to twenty years.

My first prediction is that China will continue to strive to have good relations with all small countries in its neighborhood, except those that invite in U.S. military power (for example, Thailand, the Philippines, and now Laos).

To the west, China has a border agreement with Afghanistan. On the Indian subcontinent, it has very satisfactory military and economic relations with Pakistan. In fact, in its virtual military alliance with both the West and Communist China, Pakistan has achieved the seemingly impossible. China also has excellent relations with Nepal. The two states have had a border agreement that, according to the Nepalese, gave them 900 out of 956 square miles of disputed territory.

Since the Chinese obtained only 56 square miles of the disputed land, the Nepalese were very pleased. They find the Chinese meticulous in the performance of their trade obligations and their various aid commitments and consider China the best country from which to get aid.

Ceylon, to the south of India, is also pleased with China's economic policies. Chou En-lai's visit in 1964 created an enormously good impression. Mrs. Bandaranaike, then Prime Minister of Ceylon, told him that her country was very short of textiles for the new year and wanted 25 million yards of cotton piece goods within a month's time. Could China sell them to Ceylon? Chou told her that, although China was very short of textiles itself, and although the per capita quota of textiles in Ceylon seemed to be higher than in China, he would see what he could do. The next day he told her that, not only would China supply the textiles Ceylon wanted, but it would let Ceylon have them free as a new year's gift. Ever since, Sino-Ceylonese relations have been very warm. Moreover, hard-headed Ceylonese officials have told me that, in the performance of their contracts with Ceylon, China has been absolutely scrupulous. China had an agreement to supply rice to Ceylon in exchange for Ceylon's rubber. China was not always in a position to supply its own rice and, at times, had to buy rice on the world market for delivery to Ceylon. When the world market price of rice shot up, the Chinese paid the higher world price but delivered the rice to Ceylon at the agreed contract price, thus suffering a loss. In contrast, in its beet sugar agreement with East European countries, Ceylon found that the East Europeans refused to supply beet sugar at the contract price after the world market price had gone up.

Burma, on the other hand, has had difficulties with China, although here again there is a border agreement that has generally worked very well. The present difficulties between Burma and China are partly due to the fact that the Burmese leader, General Ne Win, has been a very close friend of Liu

Shao-ch'i, the discredited ex-President of the People's Republic of China. This has been a thorn in the side of the Maoists in Peking. In some respects, relationships between Burma and China are again settling down.

In Laos, where the Communist Pathet Lao and the Lao Government have been fighting for years, China has been very circumspect. In the course of international negotiations to end the struggle, during which I got to know some of the Chinese leaders and other interested parties rather well, I was impressed by the fact that no one, not even American intelligence personnel, alleged that there were any Chinese troops in Laos fighting for the Pathet Lao, despite the fact that there were American and other troops in uniform in that country bordering China. The absence of the Chinese was not due to absent-mindedness but to the fact that China realized that it had to be very careful in its dealings with small countries on its periphery. It does not intend to behave aggressively toward these small countries, because this is not the way to obtain their respect and esteem. Prudence and circumspection will continue to mark China's relationships with them. They, in turn, will be expected not to enter into a military alliance or other such arrangement with a country unfriendly to China.

My second prediction is that China will have a difficult time with the two larger Asian nations, India and Japan, at least for the next ten or twenty years.

China does not have good relations with Japan, although it has a good deal of trade with that country. Moreover, its historical experience with modern Japan is sufficiently adverse for Peking to be rather suspicious of Japan, and there is much about Japan that it does not like. The Chinese are also very aware of Japan as a potential great power center, and they are going to be very careful in their relations with it. Much depends on whether Japan decides to become a nuclear power. If it does, there will be a very long period of bad relations between the two countries.

Although there is a long history of good Sino-Indian relations, a new set of circumstances in the contemporary period has led to Sino-Indian dissension and a short bout of border warfare. Historically, Indian influence on the whole of South Asia, Southeast Asia, and, indeed, on China itself, has been considerable. A good deal of Chinese philosophy, its epistemology, its metaphysics, and one of its main religions, Buddhism, have been imported from India. These cultural bonds have historically linked the Indian subcontinent and the Chinese world, each having about one-fourth of the world's population. In the contemporary period, however, China sees in the hostility between India and Pakistan a chance—for the first time in recorded history—to extend Chinese influence into the subcontinent. Peking apparently thinks that that influence can be maintained only by being very friendly with the smaller of the countries at the expense of the larger one. This situation makes it possible for Peking to be less careful in its relations with New Delhi than in its relations with Tokyo. Thus, the problem of Sino-Indian relations is complex, complicated still further by almost 2,500 miles of common frontier, and by the question of nuclear weapons, which China has and India does not have. If India does not go nuclear, Sino-Indian relations may improve. India, for its part, does not make bad relations between Pakistan and China the price of re-establishing relations of mutual respect with China.

My third prediction is that China's relations with the United States and the Soviet Union will also remain difficult, but that the first of these two powers with which China will mend its relations will be the United States.

There is no common Sino-American frontier. The ideological unity of the Communist world is obviously breaking up into several pieces. Even if Mao Tse-tung or someone else wanted to restore the monolithic unity of an earlier time, it would not be possible. The United States will find, therefore, that it can put ideological differences in the background.

A better Sino-American relationship is not going to come about through little gestures. The Chinese regard China as a great country and will not accept small favors from another great country. They would trade with the United States, if it suited them to do so, but they will insist upon being treated in full equality as a major power and as part of the general community of nations. They will not accept any sort of second- or third-class status or any sort of "on trial" relationship. I think that Taiwan as a problem in Sino-American relations will work itself out after General Chiang Kai-shek disappears.

Of the great powers, I am pretty sure that the last fence to be mended—if it is mended at all in the foreseeable future— will be that between China and the Soviet Union. There are wild men in all countries; they are not the monopoly of any country. If the wild people in the Soviet Union and those in China decided to fight each other, the whole world picture might be radically changed. It is, therefore, hazardous to make predictions about China, for the Sino-Soviet relationship is so bad that a further deterioration might alter the situation within China to the extent that China would no longer be what it appears to be today.

In sum, China will continue to have good relationships with its smaller neighbors in Asia. Its present difficult relations with Japan and India may improve, if neither state develops nuclear weapons. Of the two superpowers, the outlook for better Sino-Soviet relations is extremely poor; China is likely to improve its relations with the United States first. If Sino-U.S. relations do improve, while Sino-Soviet relations remain sour, Peking might well decide that it would like to work out a better relationship with Japan as well as with India. In this endeavor, China could probably count on the mediatory influence of the United States. It would be interesting indeed to see these moves for harmony among Japan, the technological leader in Asia, China, the Far Eastern giant modernizing itself, and India, the old spiritual leader of the region, synthesizing, as always, the traditional and the new. But if these peaceful developments are to take place in Asia, China will have to bring to them as its contribution a more relaxed and less competitive spirit than it has so far shown in its attitude toward the large states of Asia and toward the United States.

LADY JACKSON (BARBARA WARD)

China must be seen and understood as part of that penumbra of states, continents, and cultures that were knocked out of historical sequence by the enormous eruption of science and technology in the form of the Western world and that still bear the marks of the lopsidedness that this encounter with the West created. China, like India, like parts of Latin America, and—at a different level—like Africa, was the subject of a whole series of changes in the nineteenth and early twentieth centuries, which go far to explain many of its internal problems and external relationships today.

Put simply, China was drawn into a world economy as a suffering rather than an acting element. While it was strong, it refused open trade with the West. But as its power weakened in the nineteenth century, Britain broke open its doors with a disgraceful war designed to compel it to purchase opium. Thereafter it was, willy-nilly, drawn into the trade patterns established by the enormous need the Atlantic world felt for the raw materials and goods of the East, of Africa, and of Latin America.

This circuit of trade meant that one part of the Chinese economy—the export sector and its vast ports, Shanghai and Canton—was forcefully modernized, while modernization in the internal parts of the countryside was minimal. There was, then, a sudden juxtaposition of two ways of life, of new and old. Moreover, there were very few mediating institutions. In India, an administrative takeover by a Western power gave a certain unity of experience. China entered the twentieth century a house divided.

The "Open Door" meant that everybody could get in and bang about and bargain and invest—and sometimes cheat. At another level, missionaries could enter to lay new ideas beside the old. The result gave very little coherence to the vast Western impact on China. Its consequences are still there today, consequences that China shares with the whole of the developing world.

They are: a very belated modernization of agriculture, the creation of vast urban conurbations before there is a full industrial structure to give them their economic life, the emptying of peasants from a depressed countryside into these vast cities, and, in those cities, new Western technology designed to meet the needs of capital-intensive rather than labor-intensive industries. Along with these imbalances is a population increase spurred by the introduction of public health way ahead of other kinds of modernization, including the kinds of modernization that can give employment to a work force growing by 2 per cent a year. Mix these elements thoroughly, shake well, and you get a global Molotov cocktail. This crisis of modernization—relative backwardness in agriculture, over-urbanization ahead of industry, and the appallingly relentless pressure of population growth—obtains all around the world, and that is what the Chinese are coping with.

What are the implications of this for the Western states'

relations with China and China's relations with the world? This particular crisis of modernization will occur on continent after continent and will probably make the 1970's a time of immense turbulence. Whatever we choose to call the process ideologically, the many sources of turbulence are rooted in the actual bare confrontations of economic and social fact. Ideology is added rather like a top dressing, but the reality is underneath and cannot be wished away. It is rooted in these historical contradictions.

During the 1970's in India, in Pakistan, in parts of Africa, and all along the Andes, there will occur a working out of these insoluble pressures of population, agricultural backwardness, too-rapid urbanization, and vast migration from the countryside to the cities. These problems, these crises, will obtain quite independently of ideology. This should be understood as we confront the 1970's.

Therefore, the reason why we in the West cannot afford not to be as clearly informed about China as possible is that the way China reacts to this crisis can be of crucial importance for the whole of the human race. If China cannot master this crisis, tragedies may engulf one-fourth of the human family. Given the Western world's vast capacity to produce more food, its scientific and technological apparatus, its infinite ability to cope even with its own errors, it is inconceivable that, in a time of major crisis in Asia, with possibly massive suffering in China, our channels of communication, our understanding, our relationships should be so poor, meager, and remote that we could not in fact respond in a humane and dignified way to real disaster. Those who have already achieved, however faultily, some kind of control over their resources have both a moral and a realistic obligation to see that those resources work to speed up all around the world this really agonizing time of modernization, when the old way of life dies and the new is not yet born.

But suppose the other alternative obtains. Suppose that, in

the course of the 1970's, some of the essential factors in the crisis of modernization begin to be mastered in China. Suppose that, for instance, out of something that is now occurring— the transfer of population from cities back to the countryside, the enormous concentration on labor-intensive work in the country—comes a whole set of workable solutions to the crisis of the 1970's. What idiots we would be if we were unable to learn directly, to compare, to ask for help, to ask for the transfer of knowledge, to ask to do joint work with China in these fields.

How could we possibly cut ourselves off from a successful experiment that covered one-fourth of the human race? Whichever way the almost certain crisis of the 1970's goes, failure to have relationships with China would be tragic. They could begin modestly but be built up on the basis of good faith and on the basis of a deep desire to understand where the human race is tending in the crisis of our time and what mankind can do to master the challenge. If we fail to establish a relationship with China, we may either stand by unwillingly, but quite impotently, during a major catastrophe, or we may miss opportunities of learning and applying new policies and new approaches that could give answers to appalling difficulties that lie ahead.

Do not let us, therefore, for lack of history, for lack of understanding, or for lack of analysis, accept ideological top dressings and miss the solid substance of human fact and potential human tragedy underneath. Let us be thoroughly reasonable in our approach. Let us realize that, having in some measure got through the crisis of modernization ourselves and controlling a margin of resources for action, we would be guilty of criminal stupidity if we cut ourselves off from the one-fourth of humanity that may need our help or could help us in a major way.

When we think about China, let us think of it within this wider context of the crisis of delayed, partial, and difficult modernization and vow to use our resources creatively to speed up solutions. By this, I mean foreign aid, I mean subscriptions to the International Development Association, I mean using the resources of the World Bank and the United Nations Development Program. I mean using at least 1 per cent of the gross national product for creative development. And I mean using them in all developing lands, including China, if dignified and acceptable means of assistance can be worked out. For there is at least a chance that, if we use our wealth to do something about the real crisis of mankind, perhaps, under God, we shall manage to get into the twenty-first century.

VI.
The
United States
and China:
Policy
Options
for the
Future

JOHN D. ROCKEFELLER 3rd

I am happy for the opportunity to re-state my long-time conviction that responsible public discussion is essential to the building of a more viable relationship between Americans and the people of China, and I want to pay tribute to the important work of the National Committee on United States —China Relations. Surely these endeavors will help provide us with a firmer base on which to assess the China problem and to determine how best the United States can find a reasonable *modus operandi* with the world's most populous nation.

All of us recognize the uncertainties and frustrations in this problem. What is hard to accept is that these difficulties have managed to paralyze American processes of creative thinking. We can look back on what now seems the golden age in our relationship with China, from the time our first Consul General arrived in the 1780's up until the 1930's. Throughout that century-and-a-half, our nations enjoyed a growing sense of friendship and exchange. Yet the relationship was essentially superficial, despite many significant and genuine humanitarian efforts; as a nation, we did not really come to know China and its people. Then China's agony began. Nearly forty years later, it is still going on.

For the past twenty years, we have had no relationship with mainland China whatsoever. During this time our thinking about that great country has been so dominated by fear that in the recent past many regarded it as virtually treasonable even to raise the question of re-thinking China policy. This sort of rigidity has no place in a democracy. We must not only understand China better but we must also understand our own fears. We must come to think openly in terms of reasoned and enlightened self-interest.

It is much easier to criticize past and present policies toward China than it is to improve them. Perhaps these policies basically reflected the national mood, but what was missing was open and courageous debate. The time for re-examination of our policies is now. We must not shrink in questioning all formulas or ties that have seemed to serve us well in the past. I fervently hope that we have passed through the shadows of fear and are ready to think constructively about the future. Clearly it is time for a new look.

ARTHUR J. GOLDBERG

In a discussion of whether China policy initiatives are feasible and desirable, the main focus obviously is on mainland China. There are necessarily involved, however, implications for U.S. policy toward Taiwan and Asia as a whole. Furthermore, the border clash on the frozen Ussuri River makes it imperative that such discussions treat with U.S. policy toward the continuing ideological and military conflict between Communist China and the Soviet Union.

Virtually nothing that the United States can do in the foreseeable future with respect to mainland China will change the present unsatisfactory state of relations between these two countries. Even if the United States were to disavow Taiwan and seek to establish diplomatic relations with mainland China, nothing much or different or for the better would soon happen in United States–China relations. The extremely xenophobic character of the present Chinese regime would seem to preclude a genuine betterment of relations for the immediate future.

Nevertheless, I favor a change in our China policy. In the first place, although a short-term pessimist, I am a long-term optimist, believing as did an ancient Greek: "Nothing terrible lasts forever or even for long in the perspective of human history."

Secondly, while the lessening of tensions with China cannot be achieved solely by American acts, it certainly cannot be achieved *without* America's actions.

Thirdly, a more liberalized China policy is desirable to make clear to the international community that it is Peking and not Washington that is isolating Communist China from the world. In this context, America could begin by no longer acting as the principal barrier to the admission of mainland China to the United Nations.

Finally and fundamentally, a change in China policy is a necessary ingredient of a new foreign policy for the United States, which is also needed.

One aspect of such a policy is a return to the old principle that George Washington enunciated in his Farewell Address: "Permanent, inveterate antipathies against particular nations and passionate attachments for others should be excluded." The United States would do well in reviewing its China policy to remember this truth, particularly as the Administration contemplates the changes in the antagonisms and alliances to which the nation has become accustomed and in which it has been involved in the past twenty-five years. In the context of both Europe and Asia, old antipathies have yielded to new friendly attachments. Therefore, it would be wise to stick to Washington's rule: "Observe good faith and justice toward all nations."

I do not share all the views expressed in President Washington's Farewell Address, however. In this age of thermonuclear rockets, no nation in the world, even beyond the widest oceans, can ever again describe itself as enjoying, in his words, "a detached and distant situation." President Washington's essential theme is a wise one that, properly viewed, is not so much a counsel of isolationism but rather advice President Kennedy updated when he said: "The United States is neither omnipotent nor omniscient . . . we cannot impose our will, we cannot right every wrong or reverse each adversity . . . there cannot be an American solution for every problem."

Perhaps the difficulty in achieving viable United States–China relations is that America has been seeking an American solution for a problem that the Chinese themselves, their Asian neighbors, the world community, and time must all join in seeking to solve.

JOHN K. FAIRBANK

As a historian, I would place relations between China and the United States in a perspective that has six points.

The first perspective on China is historical. Those of us who lived there in the 1930's and 1940's recall that the charm of Chinese life was its medieval quality. Those years were a time of backwardness for a Chinese society that had achieved an early maturity and high sophistication 1,000 years ago but lacked modern technology and conveniences. Today, the Chinese are still trying to install running water and electricity throughout their countryside, and they are concentrating on internal tasks.

This internal focus has a long history. China is a country that has expanded within its own imperial half-continent. The Chinese are not primarily a seafaring people like the Europeans, nor have the mainlanders been a capitalist enterprise people. This quarter of mankind has never expanded like the European powers and set up colonies overseas. For the most part, they are self-contained, inward-focused, and content to remain at home. And they are a bureaucratic people. As a result, China plays a very small role in the modern world; its participation in international affairs is limited; and it has relatively little trade with the rest of the world.

Partly for these reasons, China has never lived up to the hopes and fears of outsiders like ourselves. Throughout the nineteenth century, the West had high hopes, which never materialized, for a sizable Chinese market. Instead, Japan became the great market that it is today. Generations of missionaries aspired, and failed, to convert the Chinese masses to Christianity. Today, Americans fear China's potential military capability. Although the Chinese have not yet launched an ICBM into the Pacific, Washington assumes that they will do so.

This point leads to a second perspective that has to do with Americans. American policy toward China is based mainly on fear. This is particularly true in the field of nuclear weapons. The U.S. idea of developing an ABM system against China, for instance, is an explosive mixture of America's high technical skill and its capacity for self-deception. Our defense specialists affirm that ours is a defensive weapon but refuse to admit that a Chinese ICBM, if they should develop one, could be China's effort to deter a nuclear attack. The error here is to assume that American defense specialists, as the Secretary of Defense has said, are not in foreign relations. They are obliged by their responsibility to prepare for the worst, and, in so doing, they make its occurrence more certain. In other words, their defense effort based on fear alone, on weapons, is no defense. This is certainly the misconception of the century. I submit that human history is a story of constant warfare, that this warfare will go on into the future in some fashion, and that, in recent decades, nuclear capability has presented a danger that is accelerating. The only answer to the problem of nuclear warfare is to place a higher value on the brotherhood of man, to refrain from polemics against other nations, and to try to get a combination of hardware and diplomacy that will deter war and encourage peace.

As a third perspective, U.S. China policy must be seen in the context of Vietnam. The Vietnam War grew out of the American policy of containment of China; it was America's attempt to contain the Maoist war of liberation. The stalemate that the United States faces in Vietnam, however, is a defeat if measured against our original purpose there. Moreover, it is hardly surprising that the American public is, on the whole, against the Vietnam War, our second biggest national disaster after the Civil War.

Senator Kennedy's speech was very courageous and an example of clear thinking. In essence, he proposed a better American posture toward China. Although the program he outlined may not be feasible for some time to come, he did set forth proposals for a better future posture. Yet he left out the Vietnam aspect of American China policy. Mr. Nixon and his administration must be helped to accept the reality of a measure of defeat in Vietnam and to reconsider our policy toward China in the light of that reality. Because the Vietnam War grew out of the effort to contain China, because that war has failed to achieve U. S. objectives and has, essentially, been repudiated by the American public, perhaps it is time to change our China policy and to make it less military and more diplomatic.

A fourth perspective also involves Americans. The American menace to mankind is chiefly in our capacity for self-righteousness and in our culture-bound and thus distorted image of the world and of our place in it.

First of all, the assumption that American policy must serve the American national interest alone is wrong. We have to consider our national interest as part of a world interest and try to coordinate it with that of other governments and the world as a whole. Abroad, the United States is often somewhat feared, somewhat admired, somewhat appreciated, and there has also been great uneasiness about our judgment. Many of the troubles we have gotten into seem to arise from miscalculation. We must listen to other countries. The deployment of our missiles, for instance, does not concern us alone, but many other states as well.

Secondly, Americans are ignorant of Chinese ways and certain that the American way is superior. Thus, we are quite willing to welcome the Chinese into our world, if they will follow our rules. President Nixon even went so far as to say in his first press conference on January 27, 1969, that Peking had not recently applied for U.N. membership. In the language of the streets, he was saying, "Look, Mr. Mao, we have only blackballed you sixteen times; why don't you apply again? If you want to join our international club, you have to follow our rules. We can bomb your ally to the south according to a rule we have that gives us the right to resist aggression anywhere. But when you claim the right to demand world revolution, Mr. Mao, you disqualify yourself." Americans must understand Chinese pride and the fact that Chinese militancy is a compensation for Chinese weakness.

My fifth perspective involves the triangular relationship of the United States with the Soviet Union and China. The nature of this relationship requires even-handed treatment of both other parties. If America supports the Russians against the Chinese or the Chinese against the Russians in the Sino-Soviet contest, it can only get itself in trouble. We must stay out. Indeed, U.S. support of the Russian side against China could force the Chinese to adopt a new pro-Russian policy.

A sixth and final perspective: The main Chinese problem is domestic. It is a problem of political organization and arises from the enormous size of the Chinese population. Mao's politics have superseded his economic program, his military program, his foreign policy. He is trying to create a modern state inside China, but he is not certain he can do it. Although Mao is a great revolutionary, he has adopted some very peculiar means of achieving this objective. However we view these experiments, American relations with China have to await China's development. The United States cannot force itself on the Chinese. The posture toward China that Senator Kennedy outlined provides the greatest hope of improving relations, the best position to assume. It offers a hand of modest friendship, in comparison to the trigger-happy approach represented by the installation of American missiles on China's periphery and the organization of a domestic antiballistic missile system directed against China.

The only answer to the cruel and difficult problem of Vietnam is in American minds. Americans must recognize the impact of the Vietnam War on our relations with China. Any chance of achieving a measure of stability in those relations depends on the settlement of the Vietnam War on terms that are in some measure satisfactory to Peking, as well as to Washington, Saigon, and Hanoi. The Chinese will probably have to be invited into the negotiations before any kind of settlement can be expected. In the meantime, Mr. Nixon's best hope of improving Sino-American relations lies in adopting the posture proposed by Senator Kennedy. The militaristic programs proposed by the Defense Department should be avoided.

THEODORE C. SORENSEN

As the Soviets and the Chinese confront each other across the Ussuri River, the United States would do well to recall an old Chinese saying: "It is better to sit on a hill and watch two tigers fight."

I do not suggest that war between these two large and bitter adversaries is in America's interest—no war anywhere in the world is. But I do suggest that it is *not* in America's interest to take sides in this dispute, to appear to take sides, to permit itself to be used by either side, or to give either nation grounds for charging that it has taken sides. I am further suggesting that, if such a stance is the right one, the United States should no longer continue its policy of making a greater effort toward understanding and friendly relations with the Soviet Union than it does with Communist China. Contrary to the basic assumptions of American foreign policy for many years, there is no foundation in fact or logic for continuing to apply a double standard to American relations with the Soviets and the Chinese. Peking may erect barriers that make impossible a relationship with the United States that is the equivalent of Washington's relations with Moscow, but there is no reason for the United States to erect any different, extra, or higher barriers between itself and the Chinese than it does between itself and the Russians.

The United States should be equally vigilant in its policies toward both nations, equally realistic about the substantive as well as the ideological conflicts that divide the United States from both nations, and equally frank about America's limited ability to intervene or otherwise influence events around the borders of both nations. I am not advocating either a regression in U.S. relations with the Soviet Union or an unseemly rush to make concessions to mainland China—only an attitude that is equally cautious, equally forthcoming, equally suspicious, or equally hostile toward both nations. The United States can no more judge the merits or predict the future course of the Sino-Soviet feud than Shakespeare's Prince could understand the Montagues and the Capulets. But whether America's cry, like his, is a "plague on both your houses" or something a little more diplomatic, it should take care not to embrace one of these two gladiators while attacking the other.

Some may reply that China is more hostile and Russia is more friendly. It is true that Peking's words have been more hostile than Moscow's and any overtures made now may well be rejected. But Moscow's deeds have been more threatening than Peking's; and surely U.S. policy in terms of what is sought, its posture, should not place more importance on words than on deeds. For, after all, it is the Soviets, not the Chinese, who are the chief suppliers of weapons used against American troops by the North Vietnamese and Vietcong. It is the Soviet Union, not China, whose forces pose a potential threat to America's at the Berlin Wall and in the Mediterranean. And it was the Soviets who tried to establish nuclear missile bases in the Western Hemisphere and who ruthlessly invaded their peaceful neighbor for merely aspiring to a greater degree of independence.

There have been, in recent years, no comparable deployments of Chinese forces outside their own borders, nor even any very serious threats against those American forces stationed on territory claimed by Peking. Nor is there any longer good reason to believe that the North Vietnamese, North Koreans, or other Asian Communists are wholly owned and operated subsidiaries of the government of Mao Tse-tung. Propaganda from Peking may be far more harsh and belligerent than the anti-American propaganda emanating from Moscow, but China, in fact, cannot now match the Soviet Union's economic, industrial, or military capability to sustain a major threat to the very existence of the United States, and that difference in capability surely speaks louder than any difference in propaganda.

Some experts may cite the opposite justification for the present double standard—namely, that the United States need not pay as much attention to the Chinese so long as they pose less of a threat to American security than the Soviets. But that is not the reasoning that today motivates the general public's distinctions between the two, nor can the American government afford to minimize, in any way, the implications of a long-range build-up in China of both xenophobic suspicions of the United States and a nuclear missile capability, a very dangerous combination.

I stress this point in the hope that placing United States–China policy in the perspective of United States–Soviet policy may make possible a more logical attitude toward both nations on the part of American public opinion. Liberals and conservatives may rationally disagree as to where the lines should be drawn in America's relations with the two Communist powers, but they ought to agree on a policy that seeks to draw the line in the same place for both of them. I do not believe the American people would be willing to turn back the cold war clock to a point where the United States broke off diplomatic relations with Moscow, sought to exclude the Soviet government from the United Nations, forbade trade relations of any kind with the Soviet Union, and refused to listen seriously to any of its disarmament proposals. But if they recognize that that would not serve the interest of world peace, it should not be impossible for the Nixon Administration to convince them that America's present China policy does not serve the interest of world peace.

If the American people are willing to have their government offer an exchange of diplomats, businessmen, tourists, and artists to Moscow, despite Soviet actions in Europe and the Middle East, then they should be willing to have a similar offer made to Peking. If they were willing to accept Senate ratification of the United Nations Charter, under which three seats—three votes—in the U.N. General Assembly were awarded to the Soviet Union and two of its subdivisions, then they should be willing to find a formula by which both Taipei and Peking can be represented in the United Nations, regardless of who ultimately controls Taiwan.

If they are willing to have President Nixon sit down with his Soviet counterpart the year after the invasion of Czechoslovakia, why should they not want him to sit down with Mao Tse-tung as well? If American businessmen believe it is right to engage in the peaceful trade of nonstrategic goods with the Soviet Union, despite the arrest of Soviet intellectuals, how can they say it is wrong to trade with the Chinese? If Moscow is invited to the next round of disarmament talks, why not invite Peking? And if America does need (which I do not accept for a moment) an ABM system to safeguard its missiles, should it not be designed to deter the possibility of attack from either of the two leading Communist powers?

I realize that no two nations, no two situations, no two potential threats to American security, are ever identical. A United States–China policy wholly apart from the United

States–Soviet policy is needed. The difference in their responses will for some time make a difference in U.S. relationships with them. But let that be their choice. In the words
of the now-rejected Supreme Court doctrine, let American
policies toward them be "separate but equal."

GEORGE E. TAYLOR

Senator Kennedy described the China policy of the Truman, Kennedy, Eisenhower, and Johnson administrations as "a war policy"—"twenty years" of "war policy." He also described it as a policy of military containment and of isolation of China, a definition that is highly irresponsible and uninformed. It was implied that American policy was based on fear and hostility and the reports of terrorized foreign service officers. It is hard to see this as a description of the last twenty years.

"Policies" is a term used to describe the ways in which a nation seeks to achieve its objectives. These have been clearly stated in American documents. During the last twenty years, certainly since July 27, 1950, the objectives were to maintain peace among independent states by taking measures to prevent aggression and to promote economic and political growth. The past twenty years have been years of mistakes but also of achievements. It is worthwhile, before considering changes in American policy, to look at what the policy has actually been.

That policy, as established by President Truman two days after the invasion of South Korea, has been to set up such forces as might be necessary to prevent any further aggression in the Far East.

The measures taken to prevent aggression have included multilateral and bilateral arrangements with powers in the Far East. To a certain extent, these measures have been reasonably successful and have provided the base from which to operate when a more severe test came in Vietnam. But this is only part of the policy. The most important part of a policy of containment of the country identified at that time as the aggressor was to build up around it viable states, reasonably prosperous areas in which there would be economic and political growth. It would be shameful to continue this discussion without giving some credit to the Presidents who preceded this one in the work that was done there. A comparison of today's Japan, the third-ranking industrial state in the world, with Japan in 1950 gives some measure of an achievement in which the United States shares. The contrast in the standard of living on Taiwan today with that in 1949 or with that on mainland China is fantastic. There has also been political stability and a certain amount of political development. The Philippines is a mixed story, but it does include very successful assistance to the Filipinos in 1949, 1950, and 1951 in devising a progressive civil and political program to get rid of the Hukbalahaps.

Although countries cannot have too much influence upon other countries, the United States has played a role in shaping the state of Asia today. There is today a strong Japan, which is not likely to resume its prewar attitudes. The Republic of Korea is developing in a way that even the most optimistic of people in 1950 would hardly have predicted. Taiwan is stable, and there is progress in Thailand, where the United States has given some assistance, and in India, where a great deal of assistance has been given. This cannot be rubbed off as a "war policy." This is an unhappy way of describing what has gone on in the last four administrations.

The purpose of military containment is merely to provide an opportunity for countries to develop. The United States has not forced its economic or military policies on any government. Small countries, weak countries have said that they did not want U.S. aid, and the United States has left them alone. Some have accepted economic but not military aid, some have accepted both, but the United States has reacted to each case with dignity and with great flexibility. The imbalance of the last twenty years is cause for pride rather than shame. The land reform programs in Japan and Taiwan are only two examples, but they are excellent models of a scientific and regular reform of land tenure systems. These programs are making possible the development of great industrial growth.

Quite frankly, there is not a great deal wrong with this policy of containment of aggression, although there have been quite a few changes in the United States and in Communist China during the last twenty years. Communist China today is a reckless, heavily armed cripple with a degree of internal insecurity and political chaos that has led some people to anticipate the possibility of the growth of regionalism, the division of the country into small pieces, and the collapse of the whole regime. This is a distinct possibility. At the same time, China has developed a nuclear capacity—that is the biggest change in the last twenty years. The United States, which has changed a great deal, too, is still deeply involved in an effort to prevent a vast shift in the balance of power in the Far East. This effort has not failed. American political objectives did not include the demolition of the North Vietnamese regime, nor do they now. Far from having failed, the United States has succeeded in many ways in achieving the basic objective of preventing a major shift in the balance of power between ourselves and the Communist states.

But the situation today is different from that at the time of the Korean War. American policies toward Communist China do not have the complete support of all of America's allies. Does this mean that our policies must necessarily be modified? The fact that the United States resisted Communist Chinese action in Korea is to the great credit of the United States and the United Nations. As a consequence of that action, the United States does not let the Chinese finish their civil war. On this, Mao is quite correct. The United States has prevented the Chinese from completing the civil war by the use of force, just as it prevents the Germans from doing the same thing. This we have to live with. It is certainly no solution to leave Taiwan to Peking's tender mercies. America is charged with having isolated Peking. The Chinese have done such a brilliant job of isolating themselves that the United States cannot compete with them. They have isolated themselves even from their former friends.

Peking, it is said, is not expansionist—do not worry. Mr. Sorensen's estimate that the Russians are by far the greater danger is correct, but they are a different sort of danger, and the Chinese do represent a threat that would have to be taken seriously if U.S. power were to be removed. So long as U.S. deterrence is there, they do not look very bad or very dangerous, but if U.S. power were to be removed from Taiwan and the western Pacific, the United States would begin a retreat that quickly would become a rout. Time, it is said, will bring Peking to maturity; this is extremely bad history.

What, then, are the changes that should be made in America's China policy? There is no harm in having trade in nonstrategic materials, but it should not be offered to Peking as a way of proving that Americans are nice people. They would accept it as a late and grudging acknowledgment by the United

States that the embargo should never have been enacted in the first place. Let us remember that the Canadian wheat assisted the Chinese army and government to survive at a time of acute internal distress, when they had lost control of large areas of the country. Alleviation of the difficulties of the Communist regime may be a small price to pay for trade, but that was the fact.

The biggest change in policy should be in the United Nations. It makes no sense to fight the balloting battle on the terms on which we have been fighting it since 1949. The United States should take the position right away that membership in the United Nations should be universal. Everyone should be brought in: North Korea, South Korea, East Germany, West Germany, and mainland China—not as the Republic of China—but under its own name, the People's Republic of China. Make membership in the United Nations automatic. When that has been done, the Charter and the concept of the Security Council should be revised. Membership in the Security Council might be determined by such criteria as financial support and military contributions to a U.N. peace-keeping force. Such a policy has its difficulties, even dangers, but the alternative, to be forced to accept Communist China in the United Nations under humiliating circumstances, is even more dangerous and would result in far more difficulties.

By taking a new approach to the matter of U.N. membership, the United States would put the Chinese Communists in a position of having to prove that they wanted world peace, that they wanted world organization, and that they were willing to contribute to it.

HARRISON E. SALISBURY

American policies toward China and the Soviet Union are amalgams of many different things. These policies have grown up over a period of years and are like incrustations that each year have new elements deposited upon them.

The United States does not often look out about the world to see whether the policies it is following bear any necessary relationship to America's general world objectives. In this postwar era, the concept of security—that is to say, security from military threats and, as it has often been defined, from Communist subversion—has been a major ingredient in American foreign policy. The elements of this can be seen wherever one looks around the world: in the various alliance systems and in the series of forts or strongholds the United States erected first around the perimeter of the Soviet Union under the so-called containment policy and then around the perimeter of Communist China.

It is only fair to describe our policy toward Communist China as essentially a military policy, one that was more the outgrowth of the Korean War than anything else, and that was a period of time when the United States was actually at war with Communist China. Viewed in that light, U.S. policy has a certain logic and a certain reason. The Vietnam War and its origins must be viewed within that concept, because that is the way Mr. Dulles and other policy-makers viewed Vietnam in the early stage. It was one flank of a generalized engagement against Communist China; it was a southern flank of a war that was fought in the north in Korea.

That was a good many years ago, and the world has moved on, the United States has moved on, and some things have changed since Korea—but American policy essentially has not changed. This is the problem. What elements in this policy, then, are valid today, what can reasonably be discarded, what new elements are needed, and, indeed, is there something new in the world that compels a rethinking of the whole problem? There is something new in the world, something that is just becoming perceptible, something that is seen in the fighting along the Ussuri River.

Essentially, today's world is one in which there are three separate powers. Two of these powers are still stronger than the third, but quite clearly China is on its way to join that company. And it has certain remarkable advantages in the race to become a superpower. These center around what is at once its blessing and also its great handicap—its remarkable population and growth power. Most of China's problems really revolve around this numbers game.

If this is a world in which there are three superpowers, if the United States and the Soviet Union know quite well their relationships toward each other, it is because they have worked them out, hammered them out, knocked heads together, and managed in one form or another to arrive at a kind of uneasy situation in which they live in the world together. Americans do not expect the Russians to attack them with their nuclear weapons tomorrow; the Russians do not believe the Americans will attack tomorrow. Both nations have come up to the brink, backed away from it, and begun to create an environment in which they can live together and work together on certain things without liking each other very much, without any very close associations, and with a multitude of conflicts. This has been achieved contrary to the dire predictions of World War II vintage. If this working relationship has been achieved with the Soviet Union, it can be achieved with China, if American minds can create a new policy. But Americans have not started to think in these terms at all.

Do China's isolation and paranoia about United States–Soviet collusion constitute a healthy situation for us? Are they consistent with America's actual security in the world? No, the situation is an extremely dangerous and unhealthy one. China's relations with the Soviet Union are very tense. The conflict between them is not the opening act of a drama; it has been played for the last ten years. Is Sino-Soviet tension in America's national interest or in world security interest? A potential nuclear war between the world's two largest states and standing armies is not a safe situation or one that the United States can happily contemplate. The United States should have an active policy designed to reduce the tensions all around China's perimeter, and it is time now to begin to create one. Mr. Sorensen has made some suggestions; Senator Kennedy has made some suggestions. There are many things we can do now.

There are policies that can be undertaken unilaterally. There is a whole series of steps that would be in America's interest and could be taken without any necessity for reciprocity or even for detailed bargaining or diplomatic discussion with the Chinese. Although most American thinking tends to revolve around diplomatic recognition and a place in the United Nations, the fact is that there can be extremely good relations between countries without diplomatic recognition. There can be a lot of trade and a lot of intercourse, and the foundations for better relations in the future can be laid. America's best relations with the Soviet Union actually occurred in the 1920's, when there were no diplomatic relations. They have never been so good since then, and they may never be so good again.

As for what can be done now, the most important single thing is to end the war in Vietnam. That surely is in America's national interest and in America's security interest, and the effects of it will unquestionably feed back into the general international situation.

Secondly, some of the military measures imposed at the time of the Korean War can be lifted. For example, the United States could announce its willingness to lift the embargo on trade in nonmilitary items. No agreement with the Chinese would be necessary. All that America has to do is to do it.

There are some things America can do to improve relations with Japan and also lessen the tensions in our relations with China. The original term of our mutual security treaty with Japan expires in 1970 and is open for renewal thereafter. One of the keys to its extension is the situation on Okinawa. Many Japanese are opposed to the continued American use of Okinawa for nuclear weaponry. This is a very important consideration in the negotiations with Japan and one of serious concern to the Chinese as well, because the nuclear weapons America has installed on Okinawa are directed not against Japan but against China. A conciliatory U.S. position on that issue could improve our relations with the Japanese and create another pre-condition for moving toward a new relationship with China.

WILLIAM A. RUSHER

Making allowances for slight differences and for new answers, there are essentially two possibilities with respect to a China policy for the United States in the coming years. One, a policy of accommodation or working toward accommodation, would be based on the hope that in time Communist China will mellow. Then there is the policy of the government of the United States, which has been called by a term I do not object to, a policy of containment. That policy is based on the belief, supported by some evidence, that this policy, for the time being and in the present mood of Communist China, provides the greatest protection for its neighbors and indeed for the world at large and produces, in addition, the heaviest internal pressures on this extremely dangerous regime.

We have heard the case for containment, the present policy of the United States, described by Mr. Kennedy, the majority whip of the Senate, as absurd. The case for accommodation is a case that is really absurd. No one seriously suggests that the regime in Peking truly represents the approximately 700 million people of mainland China or, on the basis of the latest wall posters, even any longer contends that it controls them.

Furthermore, the proponents of accommodation have not seemed altogether clear as to the strength of this entity they wish to accommodate. On the one hand, the argument over the years has been that China must be accommodated because its power was enormous and any other course was therefore unrealistic. On the other hand, critics of a policy of accommodation have pointed to the perfectly clear statements that Lin Piao and other officials of Communist China who are still in grace and communion with Mao Tse-tung have made about their intentions for the world. These statements should be dismissed, some have said, because, in point of fact, Communist China had no power to back them up. Then there has been the line of the "prophets of inevitability." Never mind how strong, never mind how weak, never mind how good or how bad, it is inevitable that the United States must deal with Communist China and indeed that it shall go on from triumph to diplomatic triumph. Year after year, *The New York Times* ran a graph that showed that each year an increasing proportion of the membership of the United Nations was voting to admit Communist China to the seat of China in the United Nations. About 1963 or 1964, however, there came a sudden sag in that graph. Then the figure hovered a bit and sagged again. The vote last fall, in the words of the Associated Press dispatch, was the most impressive slamming of the door in four years. So the prophets of inevitability, at least as far as clutching that graph is concerned, are doing less well at the moment.

Above all, one must feel a certain sympathy for the person who rises to argue for a policy of accommodation with Communist China, because there is so little cooperation from that quarter. It has gone out of its way to exhibit its contempt for the United Nations. It has gone out of its way to insult and imprison some diplomatic and consular representatives of the nations imprudent enough to recognize it and send representatives to Peking. And, it has, to put the matter charitably, made things difficult for those who would make things easy for it. This is no accident and no disease—it is built into the nature of the regime.

On balance, the policy of containment, on the other hand, has been a solidly successful policy for two decades. For one thing it has been the uniform policy of both Republican and Democratic administrations for that entire period of twenty years, including that of the late President John Fitzgerald Kennedy and, in some ways most impressive of all, the policy of Lyndon Johnson. The interesting thing is that, if Lyndon Johnson was one-tenth as opportunistic and one-tenth as self-centered as some have said he was—and I am sure he was—then the fact that he felt it necessary to maintain this policy in the teeth of the heavy political pressures to the contrary and in the teeth of the obvious advantages of an easy way out (if there was an easy way out) is, in an indirect way, a far greater testimony to the cogency of this policy than any that I might offer.

Despite Communist China's attacks on its neighbors in literally every direction, most of the rest of East and Southeast Asia today, thanks to the American policy of containment, is freer and more prosperous than at any other time in its history, which, as Professor Taylor has said, should be scored to the credit of this execrated policy.

Finally, the Communist Chinese regime itself, once hailed as inevitable, once hailed as eternal, is racked by political controversy and intermittently plagued by outright famine. It quarrels not only with its traditional foes but with its closest allies and faces a bitter and unpredictable struggle over the succession of Mao Tse-tung. Ultimately it is doomed in any case by the factor often presented as China's greatest strength: the population explosion within the country.

What are all these points—reasons for switching from containment to accommodation? Year in and year out, across changes of administration, across changes of party, across changes of situation in many respects, U.S. policy toward China has brilliantly vindicated itself. The Nixon Administration and the Congress and the American people are in no mood to change our China policy. I personally would welcome it if Senator Kennedy or anyone else would be willing to let his election serve as a referendum on the subject in 1972 or any other year.

America is supposed to favor exciting new policies. But is it really exciting and forward-looking to adopt a policy of accommodating the tottering regime of an aging megalomaniac? Is this really the wave of the future?

JAMES C. THOMSON, JR.

Where should the United States go from here in dealing with the China problem? It is useful, though not at all reassuring, to reflect on whence we have come.

Ten years ago, the distinguished Chairman of the National Committee on United States–China Relations, Professor Doak Barnett, wrote a book in which he urged an approach to Communist China that included, explicitly or implicitly, many of the initiatives that Senator Kennedy proposed in his address.[1] In 1966, Mr. Barnett joined with John Fairbank and a good many other China specialists in urging a similar approach in that memorable nationwide television seminar sponsored by the Senate Foreign Relations Committee.[2]

Meanwhile, over the past few years, a host of public-spirited

---

[1] A. Doak Barnett, *Communist China and Asia: Challenge to American Policy* (New York: Harper & Row for the Council on Foreign Relations, 1960).

[2] *U.S. Policy with Respect to Mainland China.* Hearings before the Committee on Foreign Relations, U.S. Senate, 89th Congress, Second Session (Washington: U.S. Government Printing Office, 1966).

organizations—the League of Women Voters, the American Association of University Women, the Foreign Policy Association, and the National Committee—have all conducted continuing nationwide, nonpartisan, and educational campaigns to enlighten their members and the wider American public on the complexities of the China problem. And finally, along with this list of other developments that seem so promising, the ferment on China policy and the evolving consensus so evident both in academic circles and in portions of the public have been matched by a similar ferment and similar consensus among China experts within the federal government. There is very little that separates the specialists inside the government from the large majority of China-watchers outside the government.

But what is there to show for this decade of talk about China? Washington's rhetoric has changed somewhat: President Johnson came out for "reconciliation" with Peking in the summer of 1966; Vice-President Humphrey called for the building of "bridges" to China; and there were some ginger moves on the easing of the travel ban. There were also some furtive hints from then Under-Secretary of State Katzenbach of a willingness to re-examine the trade embargo.

When I was a bureaucrat, I and my colleagues gratefully settled for such small victories as the ones I have just described —and indeed they seemed very great at the time. But once one is outside the government, reflecting a bit, reading a bit more, facing the questions of students, looking at the world with the citizen's wider view, such "victories" are a good deal less impressive.

More striking than these victories is the fact of a continuing twenty-year deadlock between Washington and Peking. More striking is the intensified isolation of one-fourth of mankind from the rest of the world—an isolation that is *both* self-imposed and externally imposed (no need to quibble about that one). More striking is the reality of nuclear-armed

Chinese and Americans locked onto a track of hostility and perhaps collision, whether locked by our "commitments," their "ideology," or something else—both parties unable or unwilling to call a halt, to somehow grope toward a different relationship. Most striking of all are the short-term and, potentially, the long-term costs to both parties of such hostility.

Americans are an inventive people who pride themselves on their skill in problem-solving. Yet the most puzzling feature of our twenty-year China posture has been its extraordinary lack of inventiveness.

What Senator Kennedy has proposed in essence is at long last a strategy of inventiveness to deal with the China problem. He has proposed a series of unilateral American initiatives toward Peking—initiatives long familiar to the consensus both inside and outside the government but initiatives that have never been undertaken by any administration.

Why have they never been undertaken? Because some years ago America's China policy became a plaything of poisonous domestic politics. Because, further, America found itself locked into the Chinese civil war; and therefore, sadly, because *any* inventiveness on China policy might be tagged as "appeasement." And, furthermore, because pitifully few politicians, bureaucrats, or statesmen were willing to run the terrible risk of departure from rigidity.

Have times changed? This conference may be one important indicator. When Senator Kennedy can say what he said to an audience of this sort, the era of timidity may well be over. And that provides, for the first time in two decades, a fair chance for a public airing of the strategy of inventiveness.

I endorse in principle the program of unilateral initiatives toward Peking that Mr. Kennedy proposed. I endorse these steps while assuming that Peking's reaction now, and perhaps for some time to come, will be rejection and denunciation. That probability must be kept clearly in mind. Such steps are nonetheless a means to a far more important objective than the preposterous thought of winning approval from Chairman Mao—namely, the objective of offering the present Chinese leadership, its internal critics, its citizenry, and, most important of all, its successors, the clear option of an alternative relationship with the United States. As long as America fails to hold out such an alternative to these people and to their successors—as long as America lives up to Mao Tse-tung's image of us—we serve only the purposes of Mao Tse-tung, not America's national interests or the interest of peace.

This new course could and should be embarked upon tomorrow or next week or next month by the present administration—carefully and systematically—as indeed it could and should have been embarked upon by predecessor administrations over the previous decade. All that is required is a clear sense of national goals, a firm executive decision at the top, and continuing presidential leadership. All, so far, have been lacking.

Three caveats in closing: First, it will be argued endlessly—and has already been argued since Senator Kennedy spoke—that "now" is not the time for such moves. If you will excuse the jaundiced comment of a former bureaucrat, that is a very old and tiresome dodge. On the question of U.N. membership, "now" was not the time a few years ago, because China was so fierce and strong and confident, and then, from 1966 on, "now" was not the time because China was so convulsed and weak and fragmented (perhaps even on the verge of collapse). "Now" is not the time because Mao Tse-tung is dead or because Mao Tse-tung is alive or because it is unclear whether Mao Tse-tung is dead or alive. "Now" is not the time because Lin Piao is up or Chou En-lai is down or Mme. Mao is sick. The moral is, of course, that "now" is never the time. To reverse the coin, the strategy of inventiveness must be a strategy for all seasons.

Secondly, there are those who will say that we cannot move

on China because of the Soviet-American relationship. The American deadlock with China is today, and has been for some time, a very great luxury for Moscow. It is high time to ease the Russians gently into a parting with that luxury. Our efforts at détente with our foremost nuclear adversary should not be downgraded—they seem to me absolutely crucial and rightly at the top of our agenda. But there must be an upgrading of that sadly neglected factor in the global power balance, namely, America's relations with China—a factor neglected in part because there have been in recent years no "Chinese" Charles Bohlens or Llewellyn Thompsons or George Kennans who could speak with force and authority for the China ingredient of a global foreign policy at the highest levels of our government. America's China policy must no longer be manufactured in Moscow nor in Taipei—nor, needless to say, in Peking. America's China policy must be manufactured in Washington to serve America's national interests.

Finally, there must be no illusions about the potential achievements of a revised China policy, even in the long run. Whatever the United States does, even with the best of wisdom and luck, may be only marginal to the ultimate outcome. America is only one of many factors in China's life and future, and China is only one of many factors in America's life and future.

Nonetheless, I simply do not see how the greatest power on earth can any longer afford to avoid playing its proper role, however marginal it may be, in helping to resolve the long-term China problem—which is everyone's problem, not just an American problem. I devoutly hope that the construction of a new China policy will be an undertaking in which Americans of both parties can work together, freed at long last from the passions of the past.

DISCUSSION

SORENSEN: I have two related questions for Mr. Rusher. First, in his closing remark he stated that the United States should not embrace the tottering regime of an aging megalomaniac. Did he have in mind Chiang Kai-shek or Mao Tse-tung? Second, Mr. Rusher stated that the government in Peking does not represent the 750 million people from mainland China. I think it would be interesting if the publisher of the *National Review* would tell us whether the government on Taiwan represents the 750 million?

RUSHER: With regard to the first question, Mr. Sorensen, I gather from the enthusiastic response of at least a part of the audience that it's really a question of you take your aging megalomaniac and I'll take mine.

With regard to the second question, I certainly think it is extremely difficult, indeed probably impossible, to talk with any confidence about anybody at the moment representing the wishes of or reflecting the opinions of the people of China.

But always constructive-minded, I will make a little deal with you. Will you join me in a public call for a full and free referendum and election in both Taiwan and in mainland China? If so, I will print it in the *National Review*.

SORENSEN: Because I believe in some of the principles advocated by the *National Review*, I never advocate interfering in the internal processes of another country.

RUSHER: Except on Taiwan.

SORENSEN: No, I am opposed to interfering in Taiwan. Indeed, I doubt that the government on Taiwan represents the people on Taiwan.

RUSHER: But in any case, no elections to find out? We are clear about that? We are not even going to call for them? (You and I cannot impose them.)

SORENSEN: I am in favor of the people of every country telling us who represents them. The United Nations has never looked to see whether Mr. Brezhnev represents the people of the Soviet Union. It has never taken a look to see who represents the governments of most of the nations in the world. I do not know how we can judge the popular mandate of the government that is in control, to the extent that any government is in control, on the mainland of China.

TAYLOR: Mr. Salisbury spoke about the unilateral steps that the United States could take vis à vis China and said that we could end the trade embargo. I assume he meant to exclude strategic materials, and I agree with that. We could also remove our nuclear weapons from Okinawa by unilateral action. But then he said that we could end the war in Vietnam by unilateral action. Did he really mean that, and, if so, would he speculate on the implications of that action?

SALISBURY: Yes, I did mean that we could do it by a more vigorous policy of negotiation than we are perhaps now conducting. I do not mean to imply that we ourselves can do it simply by declaring peace in Vietnam because we cannot.

But I do believe that a vigorous policy of negotiation, which I do trust the present administration is going to follow, should and will produce an end to that war.

TAYLOR: I think that we can expect that eventually there will be a negotiated settlement of the Vietnam War just as there was, ultimately, of the Korean conflict. A great deal depends upon the position that we take and how much the war is hurting the other side. But I would think that within a year, or possibly two, an arrangement can be made, because I think the Soviet Union does have some reason for seeing that it be brought to an end.

FAIRBANK: I have a question to ask the gentlemen who so admire our policy of containment. Do they see any relationship between containment and the war in Vietnam? Let me explain that I do. I think that the war in Vietnam came out of our containment policy. I think that the war in Vietnam has not been successful, judged by our aim of making North Vietnam leave the South alone or judged by our aim of showing that Mao's type of people's war cannot persist against our firepower. I think the war in Vietnam is still an unsuccessful situation. I used the word "defeat"—that is a bitter word. I think we have got to face words like that. Could I hear, therefore, how our containment policy has been so successful in Vietnam?

RUSHER: The policy of containment, insofar as it is now applicable in Southeast Asia, does involve the Vietnam War, and the Vietnam War does stem from it. This is precisely true. I do not think that terms like "victory," "defeat," or "unsatisfactory" necessarily achieve, however, more credence, just because one chooses to use them. But with the war in Vietnam, the question is what is the real alternative to it? With due respect to Mr. Salisbury, I heard no alternative from him, aside from a few references to more vigorous negotiations.

In Professor Fairbank's initial remarks, he stated that the Vietnam War and policy had been "repudiated by the American public." I guess I missed my *New York Times* that day, so I wanted to ask him precisely when and where they had been repudiated by the American public.

FAIRBANK: That's very easy. It was on March 31, 1968.[1]

RUSHER: What happened? The American people did nothing on March 31.

FAIRBANK: I was trying to pay a tribute to President Johnson as one of the keenest political observers of our time. The action he took in withdrawing from the presidential race was in response to a very solid American public opinion, and, in my view, he is an expert.

QUESTION:[2] Professor Thomson, how do you look at the right of the people of Taiwan to self-determination, and how do you propose to achieve it? Professor Fairbank, what is a realistic solution to the problem of Taiwan?

THOMSON: I would like to see an arrangement whereby the people of Taiwan, as well as any other country, become more free to express themselves on the form of government they want to have. I think that the realities of the situation are that such expression will be unlikely in the short run, except perhaps by coup d'état, and that itself might not reflect the will of more than a few individuals. My own hope is that eventually some form of accommodation can be achieved between Taiwan and the mainland. I am afraid that we may have to wait a very long time for that. I myself would follow Senator Kennedy in viewing the U.S. role as one of preventing the seizure of Taiwan by force or any other resolution of the island's status by force. That is central to his view, as it is to mine.

FAIRBANK: A realistic solution is for us to keep our treaty with Taiwan and not say any more than we absolutely have to about our relationship with Taiwan. That is, we should not try to define whether Taiwan is Chinese territory or

---

[1] On March 31, 1968, President Johnson announced his decision to halt partially the bombing of North Vietnam and not to seek re-election.

[2] Originating from the audience.

whether it has some other status; we should just continue to deal with that government as we have in the past.

A decrease in the militarization of Taiwan, so that it is no longer a great military base, would be perfectly compatible with this policy. In this, I am referring primarily to the 600,000-man army of Chiang Kai-shek, although we do have a staging area there ourselves. Our defense of the island can continue. Senator Kennedy proposed a neutralization of Taiwan under guarantees that would be much less expensive for them, much less of a thorn in the side of the mainland, and could be protected by the American fleet. Now the question is whether they trust us—and I am not sure whether I would trust us.

There is no reason why Taiwan cannot be the prosperous country it is today, in or out of the United Nations. I would hope to see it in the United Nations, but it can perfectly well continue outside of it. Nor is there any question of our continuing relationship with Taiwan. We are in the same boat, we have many friends there, many common interests. It is a going concern economically, and so I see no basis for turning our backs on Taiwan when we are trying to get Peking into the United Nations. The status of Taiwan is a problem for the Chinese to settle among themselves. It is not our business.

QUESTION: I represent the organization United Formosans in America for Independence. I would like to ask two questions. Mr. Sorensen, as you know, we Formosans are determined to overthrow Chiang Kai-shek's tyranny on Formosa by every means possible. If an uprising takes place in Formosa today, what do you suggest the United States Government do with the situation? Professor Fairbank, you said that the Formosan problem is our own business. But should the United States Government continue to support Chiang Kai-shek's regime, the rule of terror on Formosa maintained by secret police, courts-martial, and concentration camps?

SORENSEN: In response to the first question, I certainly agree that the United States has not sufficiently aligned itself with the principles of self-determination in Formosa. I think there is much more that we could do along those lines. If, however, your question suggests that military intervention by the United States would be in order in the event of an uprising, insurrection, or civil war on the island of Formosa, I would be very reluctant to state in advance that the United States should once again intervene in that kind of internal disruption.

FAIRBANK: I would agree. I think that America evokes a nationalist backlash whenever it intervenes and that many people in Taiwan would be very much outraged at its coming in and trying to move things around. I do not think that we Americans, as outsiders, have the capacity to do that. One could complain that we support a government that is unjust. This happens all over the world. One minor remedy would be for us to encourage a free press in Taiwan and to have more of our journalists there—and those of other countries—to report what is really going on. All we can do is try to ameliorate the situation.

QUESTION: Ambassador Goldberg has been advocating a "two-China" policy. As a matter of fact, bóth Peking and Taipei have rejected the "two-China" formula. Does his "two-China" formula substantially mean one Formosa and one China? Would such a policy not be more realistic and practical?

GOLDBERG: I think that that point is very well taken. The use of the term "two-China" policy has been confusing. The policy I advocate at the United Nations is a one Formosa (that is, one Taiwan) and one-China policy.

QUESTION: Mr. Salisbury, what in your opinion are permanent U.S. interests in East Asia, if any, and how are they to be achieved if American power and presence are withdrawn from the western Pacific?

SALISBURY: I think our permanent interest in East Asia is one of good mutual relations with China, and I think our major interest is a China that is not, for whatever reason, a threat to the world or to itself. I think those should be the objectives of our policy.

FAIRBANK: I am sure Mr. Salisbury would also agree that Japan and trade with Japan is one of our basic concerns.

QUESTION: Mr. Rusher, can the United States police the world? Has not United States as well as European diplomacy been a reaction to the Munich conference and Chamberlain's appeasement of Hitler? Thus, since then, diplomacy has been geared toward never giving in for fear of another Hitler. Wouldn't you say that this is outdated?

RUSHER: I think it is true that the disastrous experience of attempting to appease Hitler has impressed the peoples of the world, and I am not sorry that it has. I do not think that it serves, or should serve, as a substitute for intelligent modern thought on any subject, but the lessons of history are surely there to be learned, and surely we should learn them. As for the United States policing the world, no, I do not believe the United States should police the world. I do believe that, as the most powerful non-Communist nation of the world, it has a moral obligation to try to make it possible, not only in its own interest but, to use Professor Fairbank's disjunction, in the world interest, for people who do not want to live under Communism not to have to live there. Now this does not mean protecting this or that particular square yard of territory. I am talking about a general situation. Again, insofar as Professor Fairbank's comments about impressions of the United States around the world are concerned, it has been my observation—and this applies specifically in Asia—that the peoples of Asia who live outside of what is called the bamboo curtain are in no hurry at all to get behind that curtain. They are very glad to have U.S. help and encouragement in remaining free. I think it is a pity that Senator Kennedy has never visited that part of the world and found out for himself.

QUESTION: Mr. Sorensen, you and Professor Fairbank and

others have talked about China's nonaggressive, non-expansionist attitudes. What about Tibet?

SORENSEN: I am not here by any means to defend the policies or the history of the government in Peking. My actual statement was that, in recent years, there has been no deployment of Chinese troops far from their own borders similar to the Russian invasion of Czechoslovakia or the presence of the Russian fleet in the Mediterranean. All I am saying is that we ought to treat them as equals. I remember, of course, the Chinese occupation of Tibet, but the Chinese did not regard that as the invasion of an independent foreign country.

FAIRBANK: In 1904, the British entered Tibet to counter the Russians, decided not to stay, and withdrew, putting Tibet, by agreement, under the Chinese Empire. Since then, Tibet has been recognized in international law as part of China. Chiang Kai-shek also claims that it is part of China. Moreover, no other government has come to Tibet's aid with the claim that Tibet has a legal right to be independent of China.

The Mongolian people are in a different situation. Breaking away from the Chinese Empire, they got Russian protection and remained independent of China.

QUESTION: Professor Taylor, if the Chinese people were subjected to severe famine and sought food from the world community, would you support our coming to their aid by sending wheat and other staples to China?

TAYLOR: That is a loaded question and requires a loaded answer. Obviously, I would be in favor of offering wheat to China or any other country where there was demonstrated famine. I would suggest, however, that it would be in the interest of the people concerned, as well as of the donor, that conditions be accepted that would guarantee that the wheat reached those who needed it.

QUESTION: Professor Thomson, when the Chinese refused to meet the United States in Warsaw on February 20, 1969, the Nixon Administration announced its regret that it had not been able to discuss easing travel and trade restrictions. Is there any evidence that this was a sincere statement? What is your opinion of the motivation behind that statement?

THOMSON: My impression is that there is within our government a continuing tide of interest in making better use of the Warsaw channel. I gather that this was a genuine hope of Secretary of State Rogers and the people below him—a hope I think the President shared. I do believe that we were very clumsy in our handling of the Chinese Communist defector problem, and, of course, Mr. Nixon's own rhetoric in his first press conference on China on January 27, 1969, went much further in specifics than necessary in answer to a rather misty question about China. I do believe that there is within this government some genuine hope of moving forward on China policy, but I am afraid it is way down on the agenda of priorities.

QUESTION: Professor Thomson, if the United States takes up active trade with China, would we not be giving them money that might be used for Communist aggression? With regard to trade with China, what would they trade with us in exchange for our wheat, refrigerators, farm equipment, and so on?

THOMSON: Whether our money would go into Chinese aggressive purposes relates to China's sense of priorities. China's major concern is with how to run China, how to create a modern state. I would assume that most of whatever profits might flow from what will be initially the tiniest possible trade relationship if it ever develops, would go to the building of the Chinese economy. We have further learned that China is not, in its actions—despite its rhetoric—a militarily aggressive, expansionist power. So, as to whether money earned from trade with us would go for "Communist aggression," my view is that it would probably not go for such purposes. As for the items that might be traded, in the old days, we used to get hog bristles, powdered eggs, straw, wigs, and ceramic objects. Who knows what the future will hold!

QUESTION: Professor Fairbank, in July, 1966, wrote an article entitled "The People's Middle Kingdom." [3] On page 574, he said: "Communist China, how far Communist, how far Chinese, and what is the difference anyway?" After the inauguration of the Cultural Revolution, the Red Guards destroyed quantities of works belonging to the Chinese cultural heritage. Does he still think there is no difference between the Communists and the Chinese?

FAIRBANK: I am afraid that the quotation you had from me was really a rhetorical question. Perhaps I always ought to put flags around a rhetorical question. It is not to be taken quite at face value; it is supposed to raise a subject. Your question seems unexceptionable; there is a great difference between Taipei and Peking, between Communism and non-Communism, and Soviets and Chinese.

QUESTION: Professor Mehnert said that no action has been taken by the West to exploit the Sino-Soviet conflict. Is not now the time to declare a policy of nonintervention in this conflict and, at the same time, to declare that our policy is one of coexistence with both the Soviet and the Chinese Communists? Further, is it not true that the difference in our policy toward China and Russia today is a matter of timing? We accepted the reality of the Soviet Union in 1934, and it is only in the last couple of years that the American people have begun to accept the reality of Communist China. Should we not now declare an equal policy toward both Communist countries without "approving" one or the other?

SORENSEN: Yes.

QUESTION: Mr. Salisbury, if we were to start having relations with China at this time of Sino-Soviet conflict, would this not be construed as taking sides?

[3] *Foreign Affairs*, Vol. 44 (July, 1966), 574–86.

SALISBURY: I think that the Russians might make such an argument, but I do not really see how it has any logical basis. The Chinese could equally logically say that we have already taken sides, because we have relations with the Russians. I do not believe that diplomatic and trade relations mean an alliance. An alliance is what is really considered in wartime. I think that we have every right to have diplomatic relations or any kind of relations we desire with China.

RUSHER: I was fascinated by Mr. Sorensen's and indeed Mr. Salisbury's policy, which, I gather, approves of the absolutely even-handed treatment of Communist China and the Soviet Union in their differences. Their policy fascinates me because it seems to me self-evident that it is in the interest of the United States to exploit their differences and not to treat them identically. One might argue whether one would lean toward the Soviet or Chinese Communist side but that it is in the interests of all the peoples of the non-Communist world to encourage these Communist giants to worry about each other seems to me perfectly obvious.

QUESTION: We have been discussing establishing good United States–China relations and have said that China's foreign policy, at present, is indeed a juxtaposition of both ideological and national factors. China, however, interprets the Marxist-Leninist doctrine of peaceful coexistence as a temporary period prior to the overthrow of capitalist powers and also expresses its simultaneous desire for world peace, which it defines as peace in a world without capitalism. How would you relate this outlook to United States–China relations?

THOMSON: I would merely say that they have their vision, and we have ours, and neither party is going to achieve its vision. Instead, we are going to have to try and find some middle ground, some basis of compromise for a longer term of peaceful coexistence. It is a long way off. I admire their high hopes for the world—hopes not dissimilar in fervor to Jefferson's vision that the American Revolution was "intended for all mankind."

RUSHER: It seems to me that Communist China has been inveterately hostile to the concept of peaceful coexistence and indeed turned against Khrushchev and the Russians largely on this issue. Their venomous hatred of Khrushchev personally was pinned to the fact that he had had the nerve to suggest peaceful coexistence with the United States, even if it was only a propaganda maneuver. So far as I know, peaceful coexistence has never been a part of Chinese Communist policy. It is not today—and that, most definitely, as I take it you imply, reflects very somberly indeed on the prospects for United States–China relations.

THOMSON: I would like to correct that slightly. After the Bandung Conference of Asian and African States in 1955, the Chinese did go through a period in which they pressed very hard for certain principles of peaceful coexistence. They have been through other phases in which they denounced the Russians for what they regard as outright revisionism and a sell-out to the bourgeois capitalists. It strikes me that the Chinese are capable of pursuing both courses and have done so in the past. As a matter of fact, their last Warsaw invitation was one in which they urged that we sit down and talk about principles of peaceful coexistence. So it is a continuing theme in our relationship and one that both parties can pick up eventually.

VII.
Concluding
Remarks

EDWIN O. REISCHAUER

A conference such as this does not lend itself either to a summary or to a conclusion. It is too rich and varied a symphony, too full of discordant opinions as well as complex harmonies of complementary concepts, to permit a brief or clear summation. No conclusion in this sense is possible, nor can there be one in the sense of a termination of the debate, which will and should continue. This was true when the two-day proceedings of the conference came to a close in March, 1969. It is true today, some months later, as this book is published.

In the meantime, the Nixon Administration announced on July 21, 1969, a small unilateral step toward rapprochement between the United States and China. The complete ban on imports from the mainland was relaxed to permit Americans traveling abroad to bring back with them up to $100 worth of goods that had originated in mainland China. The general restrictions on American travel to China were also lifted for members of the American Congress, representatives of the

American Red Cross, newsmen, scholars, students, scientists, and doctors, though, of course, the Chinese will probably continue for some time to keep out all Americans, except for a few very special cases. A further relaxation of the trade embargo was put into effect on December 22, 1969. This relaxation allows the subsidiaries of American firms abroad to sell nonstrategic products to China and to buy Chinese products for resale in foreign markets. It also removes the $100 ceiling on Chinese goods bought by Americans abroad for noncommercial use.

Otherwise, the general conditions of March, 1969, still prevail. Americans of all sorts long for a resolution of the war in Vietnam or at least an end to American involvement in it, but how or when either of these objectives will be achieved is still not certain. President Nixon at Guam on July 25, 1969, enunciated a post-Vietnam policy of avoidance of American involvement in the internal instabilities of Asian nations, but until this country has extricated itself from Vietnam, it is not clear how it can move to this new policy. The smaller countries of East Asia remain fearful of China and troubled by multiple internal problems. The defense relationship between the United States and Japan faces a crisis of reappraisal, which, in part, grows out of differing attitudes toward the China problem. The hostility between North Korea and South Korea remains dangerous and capable of exploding into a war that could again involve both the United States and China. The status of Taiwan and the question of Chinese representation in the United Nations are still unresolved problems. Tensions along the Sino-Soviet geographical and ideological frontiers are a threat to world peace. Future developments within China remain as enigmatic as ever and fraught with dangerous possibilities. Despite President Nixon's small step toward opening our doors to fuller relations with China and a slow shift in American rhetoric, Peking appears to remain bitterly hostile to the United States and to most of the outside world. More daring American steps toward the lessening of tensions and eventual reconciliation seem unlikely before the Vietnam War ends, and significant Chinese responses to such steps seem even more remote.

While the March conference did not bring forth any solutions to the China problem, it did, perhaps by its very diversity, broaden the vision and deepen the understanding of all who participated, either as speakers or as auditors. It also revealed quite clearly one very humbling fact. We as a nation are in great need of more knowledge about this problem and a sounder understanding of its many-faceted complexities. Clearly, we have in the past made errors—sometimes grievous ones—because of a lack of knowledge and understanding. Even today, our diverging arguments grow out of uncertain facts and a still less certain grasp of how these facts fit together.

We obviously need to make more serious efforts to develop adequate expert knowledge on China, but an even greater need is for the American public to develop a broader understanding of the problems involved in our relationship with China. As a democracy, we require not just expert knowledge, but also a certain degree of popular understanding of major policy problems, if these are to be faced wisely over any protracted period of time. This has been shown time after time since World War II in our relations not just with China but with all of Asia. The reasons for our errors and failures have usually not been the inadequacy of expert knowledge so much as the lack of popular understanding that would have permitted a wise political use of what knowledge we did have.

This weakness in our society is not easily corrected. We have an educational system that is still narrowly focused on the historical experience and cultural heritage of our own Occidental branch of humanity. In this, it is better adapted to the spirit of nineteenth-century imperialism than to the "one world" we find ourselves in today. While some progress has been made at the college and university level to correct this situation, little has been done to bring primary and secondary education into the twentieth century. It will take a long time to correct this basic educational flaw, and, in the meantime, great efforts are needed to make up for our deficiencies. This is the real significance of the March conference and the measure of its success.

CONTRIBUTORS

A. DOAK BARNETT is a Senior Fellow at the Brookings Institution. Born in China, he was formerly Professor of Government and Chairman of the Contemporary China Studies Committee at Columbia University. He has also served on numerous scholarly and consultative bodies, including the State Department Advisory Panel on China and the Joint Committee on Contemporary China of the Social Science Research Council and the American Council of Learned Societies. Professor Barnett has written or edited ten books, including *Cadres, Bureaucracy and Political Power in Communist China; Communist China: The Early Years, 1949–55; China on the Eve of Communist Takeover; Communist China in Perspective;* and *Communist China and Asia.*

FREDERICK S. BEEBE is Chairman of the Board of Newsweek, Inc., and *The Washington Post.* He is a director of Tri-Continental Corporation, Allied Chemical Corporation, and Bowaters Mersey Paper Company, Ltd., of Nova Scotia. He was Vice-Chairman of the United Nations Association's National Policy Panel on China, the U.N., and United States Policy.

LINCOLN P. BLOOMFIELD is a Professor of Political Science and Director of the Arms Control Project at the Massachusetts Institute of Technology. He served in China in 1945 and, from 1952 to 1957, was Special Assistant to the Assistant Secretary of State. Dr. Bloomfield

243

is the author of *Controlling Small Wars, The United Nations and U.S. Foreign Policy: A New Look at the National Interest,* and *Evolution or Revolution?: The United Nations and the Problem of Peaceful Territorial Change.*

CHESTER L. COOPER is Director of the International and Social Studies Division of the Institute for Defense Analyses. Dr. Cooper served as a Special Assistant to Ambassador-at-Large Averell Harriman on the question of a negotiated settlement of the Vietnam War. From 1964 to 1966, he was a member of the White House staff under McGeorge Bundy, with responsibility for Asian affairs.

ALEXANDER ECKSTEIN is Director of the Center for Chinese Studies and Professor of Economics at the University of Michigan. He has worked as an economic consultant to the United Nations and, since 1962, has been a consultant to the Department of State. Since 1966, he has been a policy adviser to the Secretary of State. Professor Eckstein's publications include *Economic Trends in Communist China, Communist China's Economic Growth and Foreign Trade,* and *The National Income of Communist China.*

JOHN K. FAIRBANK is Director of the East Asian Research Center and Francis Lee Higginson Professor of History at Harvard University. During World War II, he was with the Office of Strategic Services and the Office of War Information and became Special Assistant to the American Ambassador in Chungking and Director of the United States Information Service in China. He has been a policy adviser on China to the Department of State. Professor Fairbank is the author of *The People's Middle Kingdom and the U.S.A., A History of East Asian Civilization* (with E. O. Reischauer and Albert Craig), *China's Response to the West* (with S. Y. Teng), *A Documentary History of Chinese Communism 1921–1950* (with Conrad Brandt and Benjamin Schwartz), and *The United States and China.*

WALTER GALENSON is Professor of Economics at Cornell University. Since 1961, he has been Director of Research of the Committee on the Economy of China of the Social Science Research Council. He is the author of *Economic Trends in Communist China.*

ARTHUR J. GOLDBERG is a partner in the New York law firm of Paul, Weiss, Goldberg, Rifkind, Wharton, and Garrison. He was United States Ambassador to the United Nations from 1965 to 1968, an Associate Justice of the Supreme Court from 1962 to 1965, and Secretary of Labor in 1961–62. He is the author of several works, including *AFL-CIO: Labor United* and *The Defenses of Freedom: The Public Papers of Arthur J. Goldberg.*

SAMUEL B. GRIFFITH 2ND was a Chinese-language officer at the American Embassy in Peking before World War II. After the war, Brigadier General Griffith served in Tientsin on the staff of the Third Marine Amphibious Corps and later as Commanding Officer of the U.S. Marine Forces in Tsingtao, China, and on the staff of the Commander of the Seventh Fleet. He is the author of *The Chinese People's Liberation Army* and *Peking and People's Wars* and translator of *Mao Tse-tung on Guerrilla Warfare* and Sun Tzu's *The Art of War*.

ALVIN HAMILTON, P.C., while Canadian Minister of Agriculture in 1960, negotiated the first large cash sale of Canadian wheat to Communist China. In 1961, he negotiated a long-term agreement for even larger amounts based on a short-term revolving-credit system. In 1964, he was invited to Peking to discuss trade matters with the Chinese Government.

LADY JACKSON (BARBARA WARD) is Albert Schweitzer Professor of International Economic Development at Columbia University. From 1958 to 1968, she was a Visiting Scholar at Harvard University. She has also been a Visiting Scholar at the East-West Center of the University of Hawaii. She is a member of the Pontifical Commission for Justice and Peace. Among her publications are *The Lopsided World, Spaceship Earth, Nationalism and Ideology, The Rich Nations and the Poor Nations,* and *India and the West*.

JACOB K. JAVITS is serving his third term as a Senator from New York. He is a member of the Senate Foreign Relations Committee and the Government Operations Committee. Senator Javits is a partner in the New York law firm of Javits, Trubin, Sillcocks, Edelman, and Purcell. Among his publications are *Order of Battle: A Republican's Call to Reason* and *Discrimination: U.S.A.*

EDWARD M. KENNEDY is the senior Senator from Massachusetts and the Assistant Senate Majority Leader. He serves on the Judiciary Committee, the Labor and Public Welfare Committee, the Special Committee on Aging, and the Select Committee on Nutrition and Human Needs. He is the author of *Decisions for a Decade: Policies and Programs for the 1970's*.

JOHN M. KESWICK, C.M.G. is a Director of Jardine, Matheson, and Company, Hong Kong, and Chairman of Matheson and Co., Ltd., London. He is a director of Barclays Bank, Ltd. He has lived extensively in China and in Hong Kong. During World War II, he served on the staff of Admiral Earl Mountbatten of Burma in the Southeast Asia Command.

PAUL H. KREISBERG is Director of the State Department Office of Asian Communist Affairs. He also serves as an adviser to the United States Representative in the United States–Chinese Communist meetings in Warsaw. Mr. Kreisberg served as Vice-Consul in Hong Kong and as an intelligence and research officer of the State Department in Washington.

ARTHUR LALL is Adjunct Professor of International Relations at Columbia University. He served as Indian Ambassador and Permanent Representative to the United Nations from 1954 to 1959 and as the representative of India at the Conference on Laos in 1961–62. He has also represented India at the Eighteen-Nation Disarmament Conference. Ambassador Lall has written several works, including *How Communist China Negotiates* and *The United Nations and the Middle East Crisis, 1967*.

LUKE T. LEE is Director of the Population Law Program at the Duke University Rule of Law Research Center and Lecturer in Law at the New York University School of Law. He is the author of *China and International Agreements* and *Consular Law and Practice*.

RODERICK MACFARQUHAR was Senior Research Fellow at the Research Institute on Communist Affairs and the East Asian Institute of Columbia University in 1968–69. From 1959 to 1968, he was Editor of *The China Quarterly*. Mr. MacFarquhar is the author of *China Under Mao, The Hundred Flowers Campaign and the Chinese Intellectuals*, and *The Sino-Soviet Dispute* (with G. F. Hudson and Richard Lowenthal).

KLAUS MEHNERT is a Professor of Political Science at the Institute of Technology, Aachen, Germany. He was a Visiting Scholar at the University of California, Berkeley, in the winter of 1968–69. Among his English-language publications are *Peking and Moscow* and *Soviet Man and His World*.

FRANZ MICHAEL is Associate Director and Professor of International Affairs at the Institute for Sino-Soviet Studies at George Washington University. Professor Michael was a professor at National Chekiang University in Hangchow, China, from 1934 to 1938. He is the author of *The Taiping Rebellion: History and Documents* and *The Far East in the Modern World* (with George E. Taylor).

DAVID OANCIA served on the Peking Bureau of the *Toronto Globe and Mail* in 1965–68. He received the 1967 National Newspaper Award for his coverage of the Red Guard movement. Now living in Spain, he has written a narrative of his stay in China.

RICHARD M. PFEFFER is Assistant Professor of Political Science at Johns Hopkins University. In 1968–69, he was a Fellow of the Adlai Stevenson Institute of International Affairs and a Research Fellow in Comparative Law at the University of Chicago Law School. Mr. Pfeffer is the editor of *No More Vietnams: The War and the Future of American Foreign Policy.*

LUCIAN W. PYE is Professor of Political Science and a senior staff member of the Center for International Studies at the Massachusetts Institute of Technology. He is Chairman of the Committee on Comparative Politics of the Social Science Research Council. Professor Pye was born and grew up in North China. He is the author of *The Spirit of Chinese Politics; Politics, Personality and Nation Building; Guerrilla Communism in Malaya;* and *Southeast Asia's Political System.*

EDWIN O. REISCHAUER, University Professor and former Director of the Harvard-Yenching Institute, has been a member of the Harvard University faculty since 1939. Born in Tokyo, he was United States Ambassador to Japan from 1961 to 1966. He is the author of many works on Asia, including *Beyond Vietnam: The United States and Asia; The United States and Japan; Wanted: An Asian Policy; Ennin's Travels in T'ang China;* and *Japan, Past and Present.*

JOHN D. ROCKEFELLER 3RD is Chairman of the Rockefeller Foundation, the Population Council, the Asia Society, and the Agricultural Development Council. He is also President of the John D. Rockefeller 3rd Fund and the Japan Society. Much of Mr. Rockefeller's philanthropic work has been directed toward the development of Asia.

CHESTER RONNING was born in China. From 1945 to 1949, he was Counselor of the Canadian Embassy in Chungking and Nanking, and, from 1949 to 1951, he served as Chargé d'Affaires in Nanking. He was Director of Far Eastern Affairs in the Canadian Department of External Affairs from 1951 to 1953. He then served as Ambassador to Norway and Minister to Iceland from 1954 to 1957, and as Canadian High Commissioner to India from 1957 to 1964. He headed the Canadian delegations to the Korean Conference (1954), the Laos Conference (1961–62), and the Colombo Plan Conference (1969).

ROBERT V. ROOSA is a partner of Brown Brothers Harriman in New York and a Director of Fleming-Suez, Ltd. He is a member of the Board of Visitors of the Department of Economics of Harvard University. From 1961 to 1964, he was Under Secretary of the Treasury for Monetary Affairs. He is the author of *The Dollar and World Liquidity.*

WILLIAM A. RUSHER is Publisher of the *National Review*. Previously, he practiced law in New York City and served as Associate Counsel to the Senate Internal Security Subcommittee. Mr. Rusher is Chairman of the Political Action Committee of the American Conservative Union and is the author of *Special Counsel*.

HARRISON E. SALISBURY has been an Assistant Managing Editor of *The New York Times* since 1964. Mr. Salisbury was *New York Times* correspondent in Moscow from 1949 to 1955 and received the Pulitzer Prize in 1955 for his coverage of the Soviet Union. In 1966 and 1967, he wrote a series of articles from Vietnam and the periphery of China, for which he received the Asia Award of the Overseas Press Club. Mr. Salisbury is the author of *The Nine Hundred Days: The Siege of Leningrad; Orbit of China; Behind the Lines—Hanoi*, and *War Between Russia and China*.

THEODORE C. SORENSEN is a partner in the New York law firm of Paul, Weiss, Goldberg, Rifkind, Wharton, and Garrison. He has served as Visiting Lecturer in Public Law and International Affairs at Princeton University and has been an Editor-at-Large of the *Saturday Review* since 1966. From January, 1961, to February, 1964, he served as Special Counsel to the President. Between January, 1953, and January, 1961, he was assistant to Senator John F. Kennedy. Mr. Sorensen is the author of *The Kennedy Legacy, Kennedy*, and *Decision-Making in the White House*.

GEORGE E. TAYLOR is Chairman of the Department of Far Eastern and Slavic Languages and Literatures and former Director of the Far Eastern and Russian Institute at the University of Washington. During World War II, Professor Taylor served as Deputy Director of the Office of War Information in charge of Pacific Operations. From 1945 to 1946, he was Acting Director of the State Department's Office of Information and Cultural Relations for the Far East. He is the author of *America in the New Pacific, The Taiping Rebellion, Changing China, The Struggle for North China*, and *The Philippines and the United States: Problems of Partnership*.

JAMES C. THOMSON, JR. is an Assistant Professor of History at Harvard University and a Research Fellow at the Institute of Politics in Harvard's Kennedy School of Government. In 1963, Mr. Thomson became special assistant to the Assistant Secretary of State for Far Eastern Affairs. In 1964, he moved to the National Security Council staff, where he served as an East Asia specialist under McGeorge Bundy and Walt W. Rostow. He is the author of *While China Faced West: American Reformers in Nationalist China, 1928–37*.

Lois Dougan Tretiak is an editor of books dealing with contemporary Chinese law and politics, and a former Assistant Editor of the *Far Eastern Economic Review* (Hong Kong), writing regularly on Chinese politics and trade.

Richard L. Walker is Director of the Institute of International Studies and James F. Byrnes Professor of International Relations at the University of South Carolina. He served as a Chinese interpreter during World War II and was an Assistant Professor of History at Yale University prior to moving to South Carolina. In 1954–55, he was a Visiting Professor at National Taiwan University, to which he returned in 1965–66 as a Visiting Fulbright Research Scholar. Professor Walker is the author of ten books, including *Ancient China, The China Danger,* and *China Under Communism.*

Allen S. Whiting is a Professor of Political Science and an Associate at the Center for Chinese Studies of the University of Michigan. From 1962 to 1966, he served in the State Department as Director of the Office of Research and Analysis for the Far East; from 1966 to 1968, he was Deputy Consul General in Hong Kong. Professor Whiting is the author of *China Crosses the Yalu: The Decision to Enter the Korean War; Soviet Policies in China, 1917–1924;* and *Dynamics of International Relations* (with Ernst B. Haas).

Kenneth T. Young is the President of the Asia Society. He has spent many years in Asia both as a student and with the Foreign Service. From 1961 to 1963, he was United, States Ambassador to Thailand. He is the author of *Negotiating with the Chinese Communists* and *The Southeast Asia Crisis.*